The Songwriter's Workshop

lee

HIT SONG FORMS

PLAYBACK+
Speed • Pitch • Balance • Loop

To access audio visit:
www.halleonard.com/mylibrary

Enter Code
1825-1442-5319-7021

Jimmy Kachulis

Recording Singer, Keyboardist, and Producer: DREION

BERKLEE PRESS

Editor in Chief: Jonathan Feist

Senior Vice President Pre-College, Online, and Professional Programs/
CEO and Cofounder of Berklee Online: Debbie Cavalier

ISBN 978-0-87639-226-3

Berklee Press

1140 Boylston Street • MS-855BP
Boston, MA 02215-3693 USA

Visit Berklee Press Online at
www.berkleepress.com

Berklee Online

Study music online at
online.berklee.edu

DISTRIBUTED BY

HAL•LEONARD®
7777 W. BLUEMOUND RD. P.O. BOX 13819
MILWAUKEE, WISCONSIN 53213

Visit Hal Leonard Online
www.halleonard.com

Berklee Press, a publishing activity of Berklee College of Music, is a not-for-profit educational publisher.
Available proceeds from the sales of our products are contributed to the scholarship funds of the college.

CONTENTS

ACKNOWLEDGMENTS

Thanks to all of the following:

Debbie Cavalier, at Berklee, for her initial vision of this series, and her unstinting support through all its various incarnations. From the beginning to the end, her ideas were always crucial to its completion.

Jonathan Feist, at Berklee Press, whose insights into structuring the subject matter and focusing the topics and writing style have contributed immeasurably to this series. The series' success is due in large part to his continual creative input.

Jack Perricone, chair emeritus of the Berklee Songwriting Department, for his insights into the way songs work.

Pat Pattison, Professor of Songwriting at Berklee, for starting the whole lyric writing program at Berklee, and for his staggering insights into lyric structure and content. His books on lyric writing are an inspiration to countless songwriters worldwide. Without his dedication and inspiration, none of what we do as songwriting teachers would be possible.

Jon Aldrich, Professor of Songwriting at Berklee, whose encouragement and insights into the writing process have been a continual delight, and also for allowing me to use one of our co-writes: "Shelter Me from the Storm."

Shane Adams for his continuing inspiration and allowing me to use one of our co-writes: "The Road Remains the Same."

DREION for his wonderful performances and production of the audio tracks, making a great contribution to the success of this project. See more of his wonderful work at www.dreion.com.

All my colleagues in the Berklee Songwriting Department who have shared countless insights into the process of songwriting.

All my students—past, present, and future—who gave me their trust as a teacher. If they only knew that I learn much more from them than they ever learned from me.

Most of all, Anne, Maria Terese, and Anye for their love and understanding. Without them, none of this would have been possible.

INTRODUCTION

Welcome to the *Songwriter's Workshop: Hit Song Forms.*

ABOUT THIS BOOK

There are four units in this book: three on the standard song forms, and the last one on some new, surprising forms. Each unit has a number of songs, moving from the simplest to the more challenging forms, demonstrating the skills and tools to create that song type, and presenting suggested listening lists of hit songs that use the technique being discussed.

There are two types of hit song listening suggestions:

- examples of the full song form

- examples of the current lesson's tools (not necessarily the full song form as well)

Sidebars provide additional information about the tools.

At the end of each lesson, you'll get a chance to use the tools you learn. You'll see writing exercises with directions at each of the following levels:

1. **Practice**, the easiest exercise level, directs you to practice the tools of the lesson by setting either my lyric or your original lyric to an original melody over the provided rhythm-section track, without my melody. *Duplicate the phrasing and rhyme scheme of the original melody.*

2. **Rewrite the Hits** directs you to practice the tools of the lesson by setting your original lyric and melody over a form or chord progression based on another song—either one of the "hits" that I suggest in the lesson or any song you choose. Duplicate the phrasing and rhyme scheme of the original. This is the way the pros often write. They take a hit song and use songwriting tools to create a new song that is somehow based on that hit.

3. **Write Your Own Song** directs you to create every song element—melody, harmony, lyrics, and form—using the tools of the lesson.

4. **Challenge** gives suggestions for taking the song further, such as:

    - completing an entire song with all the sections

    - adding additional sections, like bridges, to the structure being discussed

    - creating new variations of that form that are starting to be used in more recent hit songs

To accompany your original songwriting work, you can use:

- the provided track, based on the song or song section discussed in the lesson (but without the vocals)

- your own accompaniment track (which may vary from the lesson song), which you play on your instrument or create using a software groove generator

- a produced accompaniment/karaoke/remix track to another song (such as one of the suggested hits) from wherever you like

Each form type and concept is featured in my original song examples, presented as both notation and as audio recordings. So, whether you can read music or not, you can hear the effects of that lesson's tools. *You don't need to read music to understand the effects; just listen.*

The **appendices** give references to all the key colors and chords you'll read about. Each key color has the chords in the key and power progressions for that key. There is a chart for parallel keys and another for relative keys.

If you feel the need for more guidance in those areas, this book works well with, and can build upon, the tools found in my other books in this series, *The Songwriter's Workshop: Melody*, and *The Songwriter's Workshop: Harmony* (Berklee Press). All the melody and harmony topics referenced here are described in detail in those books, as well as them having exercises to teach you how to use those tools. All three books are used as textbooks at Berklee and other institutions worldwide. Also, *Essential Songwriter* is a convenient reference and summary of many of the ideas presented in this series, intended as a quick resource of ideas to assist you during your writing process.

 ## About the Audio

To access the accompanying audio, go to www.halleonard.com/mylibrary and enter the code found on the first page of this book. This will grant you instant access to every example. These performances might vary slightly from the notation shown, with some additional nuances and flourishes added for expressive purposes (as real music does), but they show the essential concepts at work in a realistic musical context. Examples with accompanying audio are marked with an audio icon. Some practice examples have multiple associated tracks, letting you either focus on writing just one song section or incorporating that section into a larger song form context.

ESSENTIAL CONCEPTS OF SONGWRITING AND SONG FORM

In this book, you'll learn how the great songwriters choose and create the forms of their songs. Choosing the most effective song form for your song is a skill like the others you've learned: how to create melodies, harmonies, and lyrics. Now, you'll learn how to set those great ideas in the best, most memorable structures.

There are two general approaches to form:

- Create a particular song section you decide in advance: a chorus, verse, bridge, etc.

- Create a section and then decide how it fits into a whole song.

In this book, we'll use the first approach, to help you get a feel for the strengths of each song form.

Throughout this exploration, one of the most important concepts to keep in mind is the intimate connection between the music and the lyrical emotion. This is crucial: the emotion of the lyric has to be reflected in the emotion of the music. The lyric story has to be reflected in the key color, tempo, groove, melody, harmony, and form.

You will learn the strengths of each song form and how to choose the most effective one for each song you write.

Three Stages of Creating a Song

You will use your songwriting tools to:

- **create ideas**: to *generate* ideas that have melody, harmony, and lyrics

- **build sections**: to *develop* your ideas into sections (verses, choruses, bridges, verse/refrains, prechoruses)

- **contrast and connect sections**: to maintain interest in the song's narrative and emphasize the song's essential theme

Tools Produce Effects

In songwriting, we use melody, harmony, lyrics, and form to create the following three effects:

1. **Emphasis**. The songwriting tools are often used to draw attention to the important points of the lyric story.

2. **Standard Moves/Surprising Moves** (variation tools). *Standard moves* satisfy your audience in ways they expect. *Surprising moves* satisfy your audience in less predictable ways. Once you learn the standard moves, you'll learn how to create surprising moves by:

   - adding something

   - subtracting something

   - replacing something

   - stacking smaller structures to create larger ones

3. **Intensity Flow**. Learning where and how to build up and break down dramatic intensity is the last of the essential skills you need for your toolbox. It can happen either *within* a section, or *between* sections.

Creative Process

The creative process is a circular process where you use your songwriting tools to:

- generate ideas

- assess these ideas you create: keep what you want, throw out what you don't

- revise and improve your song by generating better ideas that help reinforce the song's overall intent more effectively

Like this:

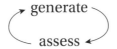

FIG. I.1. Generate/Assess

In this book, you will practice creating song sections in different orders: sometimes creating the chorus first, sometimes the verse, etc.

Audience Dynamic

When creating a song, try keeping the listener's experience of it in mind. Do you want the audience to be:

- listening to it?

- singing along with it?

- dancing to it?

...or any combination of these?

These choices can influence everything about the song: the melody, harmony, rhythmic groove, what you sing about—and just as importantly, *what song form you choose.*

Keep your audience in mind whenever you write.

SONGWRITING REVIEW

Lyrics

Lyric Emotion

There are two general categories of lyric emotion in well-written lyrics:

- **Main** or **central emotion** is told to the audience in a refrain line or chorus.

- **Supporting emotion** is shown to the audience in the non-title sections, such as verses, prechoruses, and bridges.

Show and Tell

One of the most effective ways to engage your audience in verses, bridges, and prechoruses is to *describe* scenes, characters, and emotions. This type of sensory description *shows* your audience the central emotion of the song. Try engaging these senses: sight, sound, smell, taste, touch, weight, motion.

Once they're engaged, you can then *tell* them what you're feeling in the refrain line and/or the chorus.

Groove

Tempo

Choosing the best tempo is an essential skill for your songwriting. The same lyric song at different tempos often feels completely different. Some general tempos are: slow, ballad, moderate, medium, fast, and very fast.

Feel

In addition to the tempo, the style of a song also greatly influences the way the audience experiences your lyric. Many of these are connected to different musical styles and the lyric emotions those styles express.

Some of the most common styles include:

- Rock (even or shuffle)
- R&B
- Pop
- Reggae
- Hip-Hop
- Heavy Metal
- Blues

For every song you create, make sure you're clear about the choice of tempo, feel, and groove. Here are some common descriptions:

- Slow Ballad
- Medium Blues Shuffle
- Medium Even Eighth-Note Reggae
- Moderate Hip-Hop
- Fast Eighth-Note Rock

Changing any of these can change the emotion of the song.

Harmony

Five Key Colors

There are five common key colors that you can use to express the central emotion of a song. The five basic key colors with their general emotional states are:

- **Major**: happy, optimistic
- **Minor**: sad, depressing
- **Mixolydian**: major with a little darker, bluesy feeling
- **Dorian**: minor with a little more brightness
- **Blues**: major and minor blues—a unique blend of happy and sad feelings

If we lay them out on a line from the brightest to the darkest, it looks like this:

FIG. I.2. Key Colors: Bright to Dark

Blues has its own special set of emotions, which are more difficult to describe.

Chord Colors

Within each of the five key colors, there are also mixes of major, minor, and diminished chord colors. Each of these, with its own special variations, can bring out even more subtle emotions within the broad emotions we have been discussing.

STANDARD SONG FORMS

Here are the standard song forms you'll learn how to create (and vary) in this book. Each standard song form is built from the following types of sections:

- **Verse** shows the emotion, often using sense specific language. It reoccurs with new lyrics.

- **Verse/refrain** is a verse that has the title, or refrain line, in it.

- **Chorus** summarizes the lain lyric emotion and meaning. It reoccurs with the same lyrics.

- **Bridge** a contrasting section that occurs after the second verse, verse/refrain, or chorus.

- **Prechorus** connects the verse to the chorus.

Verse/Refrain Form

A *verse/refrain* is a lyric form that has the title in the verse. There are two general types:

- **Simple verse/refrain without a bridge**. Verse/refrain songs usually just have one long musical section that's repeated over and over.

Verse 1/Refrain	Verse 2/Refrain	Verse 3/Refrain

Listen

Hit songs in a verse/refrain form include:

- Bob Dylan: "Blowin' in the Wind," "The Times They Are a-Changin'"

- Sting: "Russians"

- Simon and Garfunkel: "Sound of Silence"

- Chuck Berry: "No Particular Place to Go"

- Willie Nelson: "Blue Eyes Crying in the Rain"

- **Verse/refrain with a bridge**. More often, a verse/refrain song has a contrasting bridge after the second verse/refrain to add more interest. That is then followed by the third verse/refrain. It's described by the musical analysis AABA.

Verse 1/Refrain	Verse 2/Refrain	Bridge	Verse 3/Refrain

Listen

Hit songs that are in a verse/refrain form with a bridge include:

- The Beatles: "Yesterday," "I Feel Fine," "Something"
- Harold Arlen and Yip Harburg: "Over the Rainbow"
- Billy Joel: "New York State of Mind"
- Whitney Houston: "Saving All My Love for You"
- Lionel Richie: "Endless Love"
- Muddy Waters: "I Just Want to Make Love to You"
- Green Day: "Wake Me Up When September Ends"
- Adele: "Make You Feel My Love"

Verse-Chorus

A *verse-chorus* song alternates verse sections with chorus (sing-along) sections like this:

Verse 1	Chorus	Verse 2	Chorus	Verse 3	Chorus

Again, to keep it interesting, you can add a bridge after the second chorus.

Verse 1	Chorus	Verse 2	Chorus	Bridge	Chorus

Some standard verse-chorus songs follow the following variations:

Verse 1	Chorus	Verse 2	Chorus	Bridge	(optional Verse 3)	Chorus

(optional Verse 1)	Verse 2	Chorus	Verse 3	Chorus	Bridge	Chorus

(optional Chorus)	Verse 1	Chorus	Verse 2	Chorus	Bridge	Chorus

Listen

Hit songs in a verse-chorus form, both with and without a bridge include:

- Katy Perry: "Unconditionally"
- Sam Smith: "Stay with Me"
- Script, feat. will.i.am: "Hall of Fame"
- Smokey Robinson and the Miracles: "Tracks of My Tears"
- The Police: "King of Pain"
- Bob Dylan: "I Shall Be Released"
- Rihanna: "We Found Love"
- Bruno Mars: "Marry You"
- The Beatles: "She Loves You"
- James Taylor: "Fire and Rain"

Verse-Prechorus-Chorus

A *verse-prechorus-chorus* song has a section between the verse and the chorus, usually to build intensity into the coming chorus. Lyrics to the prechorus can repeat, or change, as you like. The overall form is:

Verse 1	Prechorus 1	Chorus	Verse 2	Prechorus 2	Chorus

Sometimes, a bridge is set after the second chorus.

Listen

Hit songs with a prechorus include:

- Maroon 5: "Payphone"
- Katy Perry, feat. Snoop Dogg: "California Gurls"
- Peter Gabriel: "Shaking the Tree"
- Whitney Houston: "How Will I Know"
- Lee Brice: "I Drive Your Truck"
- Foreigner: "I Want to Know What Love Is"
- Michael Jackson: "Billie Jean"
- The Eagles: "Best of My Love"
- Earth, Wind & Fire: "Boogie Wonderland"
- Queen: "Another One Bites the Dust"
- Huey Lewis & the News: "If This Is It"

There are a four types of prechorus songs you'll learn in unit III:

- **Loop song**, where the same or a similar progression is used in all three sections
- **Modified-loop song**, where the loop is used in two of the three sections
- **Classic prechorus song**, where all three sections are on different progressions
- **Modulating prechorus song**, where song sections are in different keys

Surprising Forms

Surprising forms are variations on the standard forms, combining them in various ways. There are a few common ones.

Verse/Refrain with a Chorus

This form combines a verse/refrain with a sing-along chorus. In this form, the title is included as a refrain line in the verse, and then used again in the chorus. The usual form is:

Verse 1/Refrain	Verse 2/Refrain	Chorus	Verse 3/Refrain	Chorus

Compare it to the AABA song form, and notice that it ends with a chorus instead of the third verse/refrain.

Listen

Hit songs that combine a verse/refrain with a chorus include:

- The Beatles: "All My Loving"
- Willie Nelson: "On the Road Again"
- Justin Bieber: "Mistletoe"
- Leonard Cohen: "Hallelujah"
- Stevie Wonder: "Signed, Sealed, Delivered (I'm Yours)"
- Bob Dylan: "Forever Young"
- Badfinger: "Without You"
- Kelly Clarkson: "Breakaway"

Two Choruses

This has two different independent choruses that can be used in various combinations.

Listen

Hit songs with two choruses include:

- The Beatles: "She Loves You"
- John Legend: "All of Me"
- Kelly Clarkson: "Since You've Been Gone"
- Katy Perry: "Teenage Dream"

Unit I.

Verse-Chorus Songs

In this unit, you'll learn the various approaches to creating a simple verse-chorus song: how to create and develop central ideas and supporting ideas into verses, choruses, and bridges. Then you'll learn how to connect and contrast the sections to create a complete song.

Loop Verse-Chorus with a Bridge ("Roller Coaster Ride")

In this, the simplest verse-chorus song type, you'll learn how to create and develop melodic ideas that connect and contrast sections over a repetitive two- or four-bar *loop* (a repetitive chord progression or a one-chord groove).

Listen

Hit songs in the simple verse-chorus-loop form include:

- Michael Jackson: "Don't Stop"
- Bob Marley: "No Woman, No Cry"
- Rihanna: "We Found Love"
- Maroon 5: "Girls Like You"
- Justin Bieber: "One Less Lonely Girl"
- Bob Dylan: "I Shall Be Released"
- Marvin Gaye: "Let's Get It On"
- Taylor Swift: "Stay Stay Stay"
- Lynyrd Skynyrd: "Sweet Home Alabama"
- Sam Smith: "Stay with Me"
- Little Walter: "Mellow Down Easy"
- Bruno Mars: "Marry You," "Just the Way You Are"

SIMPLE LOOPS

Another way to create a loop is to use a simple loop on the I chord, with variations (e.g., C7sus4 C7).

Lesson 1. Title Choruses

Title choruses are characterized by simple dramatic settings of a repeated title.

Listen

Hit songs in a simple verse-chorus form that use title choruses include:

- Bob Dylan: "Knockin' on Heaven's Door"
- Rihanna: "Disturbia"
- Aretha Franklin: "Chain of Fools"
- Leonard Cohen: "Hallelujah"
- Lee Ann Womack: "I Hope You Dance"
- Bruce Springsteen: "Born in the USA"
- Marvin Gaye: "Let's Get It On"
- The Beatles: "You've Got to Hide Your Love Away"
- Bob Marley: "No Woman, No Cry"
- Maroon 5: "She Will Be Loved"
- The Police: "Spirits in the Material World"

Title ideas summarize the central lyric idea or emotion, and a title chorus presents this in the simplest, clearest way. Two common structures for title choruses are featuring the title twice (TT) or featuring it four times (TTTT). As such, you can use all kinds of musical tools to dramatically emphasize these lyrics.

Listen to the title chorus for "Roller Coaster Ride," and notice how:

- It is in a minor key, to reflect the struggle of the relationship.
- The lyric repeats the title (setting it two times) over a repetitive two-bar loop on a Imin IVmin progression, making it a TT standard chorus type.
- It has a melodic "hooky" bass line riff.

First, here's the riff.

FIG. 1.1. "Roller Coaster Ride" Riff

Here's the chorus.

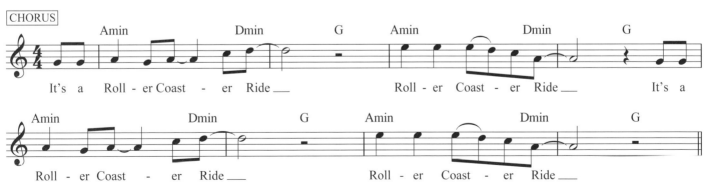

FIG. 1.2. "Roller Coaster Ride" Chorus

Listen again, and notice that the title melody emphasizes the title using the following tools:

- long notes, space, an early downbeat ending
- the two-measure idea—the melodic phrases are the same length as the chord loop
- the title is repeated both exactly *and* varied

When you have a melodic bass line like this, you can use counterpoint. In this case:

- parallel motion (phrases 1 and 3) creates the most emphasis
- contrary motion (phrases 2 and 4) is another way to create a melody over a melodic bass

TYPES OF COUNTERPOINT

The four types of counterpoint are:

1. **Parallel motion**, where both melodies move in the same exact directions, with the same intervals between voices
2. **Similar motion**, where both melodies move in the same melodic directions, but with varying intervals between voices
3. **Contrary motion**, where the two melodies move in opposite directions
4. **Oblique motion**, where one melody is stationary and the other melody moves around

WRITING EXERCISES

In each of the following, try repeating the title exactly and/or varying it, and notice the difference in feeling.

Practice

3

Set an original title to an original melodic idea, and repeat it two or four times over this loop.

Rewrite the Hits

Take a loop from a hit song, and create your own variation of it. Sing your own title two or four times over it.

Write Your Own Song

Create an original two- or four-measure loop, and sing your own title two or four times over it.

Lesson 2. Standard Verses

Verses use lyric ideas that support the central lyric idea of the chorus. Musically, verses are usually more conversational and less dramatic than choruses. They often *show the story* using sense-specific, descriptive language. In a verse-chorus loop song, the same chord progression loop is used for all the sections.

A *standard verse* has four two-bar phrases with the rhyme scheme such as aabb (or aaaa, abab, or xaxa). "Roller Coaster Ride" uses an aabb structure for the verse phrases, which can be analyzed like this:

	Number of Measures	Rhyme Scheme
*You lean in close then you push me **away***	2	A
*You're jumpin' out then you beg me to **stay***	2	A
*We hold each other through the tunnel of **love***	2	B
*My mind is reelin' and I've had **enough***	2	B

Listen

Hit songs the use the standard rhyme schemes in the verses include:

abab or xaxa

- The Rolling Stones: "Honky Tonk Women"
- Tina Turner: "Private Dancer"
- The Beatles: "She Loves You"
- Merle Haggard: "Okie from Muskogee"
- Lady Gaga: "Paparazzi"
- Katy Perry: "Unconditionally"
- Train: "Hey Soul Sister"
- The Police: "Every Little Thing She Does Is Magic"
- Bob Dylan: "I Shall Be Released"
- Joni Mitchell: "Circle Game"

aaaa or aabb

- The Police: "Message in a Bottle"
- Muddy Waters: "I'm Your Hoochie Coochie Man"
- Willie Nelson: "My Heroes Have Always Been Cowboys"
- Bruce Springsteen: "Hungry Heart"
- Sam Smith: "Stay with Me"
- John Mayer: "Daughters"
- Jess Glynne: "I'll Be There"
- Maroon 5: "She Will Be Loved"
- Katy Perry: "Hot 'n' Cold"
- Justin Bieber: "Baby"
- Lady Gaga: "Applause"

Listen to this standard verse from "Roller Coaster Ride," and notice that it includes:

- four two-bar phrases (2222) with the rhyme scheme aabb
- the same chord loop as the chorus, on the chords Emin Amin D (see figure 1.1)
- short, conversational word rhythms, range in the lower register, a simple minor-blues pentatonic scale, and variations of one basic rhythmic idea

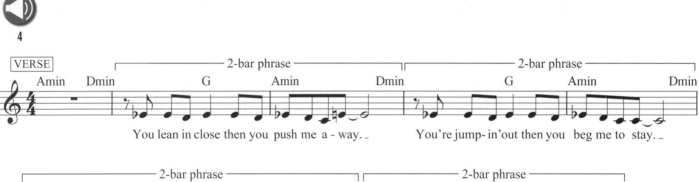

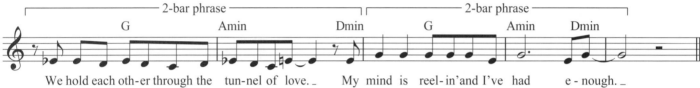

FIG. 1.3. "Roller Coaster Ride" Verse

Listen again, and notice how the melody ends with a new idea that is higher (which builds intensity into the coming chorus).

COUNTERPOINT CONTRAST

If you use a melodic bass line with your loop, try using a different type of contrapuntal motion in your melody. Notice how this melody contrasts with the active bass line by staying around one area (*oblique motion*).

Additional notes:

- The verse uses the same harmony as the chorus (see lesson 1). Together, they form a simple *verse-chorus loop song*.

- The standard lyric rhyme schemes are: aaaa (aabb) or abab (xaxa). Note that aaaa and aabb can be used interchangeably within a song or section, as can abab and xaxa.

WRITING EXERCISES

To practice using these tools, do any of the following exercises. Use one of the standard lyric models in this lesson and short conversational rhythms, in the lower range of your voice.

Practice

5

Set your original lyric or this lyric verse over an original melody on this loop.

Rewrite the Hits

Set an original lyric over a loop from a hit song.

Write Your Own Song

Create an original verse melody and lyric over the original loop you used in lesson 1.

Challenge

Write a rap verse with a more traditional chorus. Some call this *melodic rap* or other names. This can maximize the audience for your song, creating two types of verses:

- a rap verse that uses the high and low pitch of traditional rap
- a more conventional verse that uses more pitches to give it a more "melodic" feel

Listen

Hit songs that have a rap verse include:

- Nicki Minaj: "Fly"
- Kesha: "Your Love Is My Drug," "Tik Tok"
- Ed Sheeran: "Galway Girl"

Note: You can use a rap verse in *any* of the song forms you will learn here.

Lesson 3. Contrast and Connect: Verse to Chorus

When creating a verse with a chorus, there are a few central principles:

- *Connect* the sections.
- *Contrast* the verse with the chorus.
- *Build intensity* at the end of the verse.
- Create dramatic *emphasis* in the chorus. The chorus should be the emotional high point of the song.

Consider the "Roller Coaster Ride" verse and chorus together, and notice the ways that this simple verse-chorus song achieves all those effects.

- The end of the verse *builds intensity* and *connects* to the chorus.
- The verse *contrasts* melodically with the *more dramatic* chorus.
- The end of the chorus will connect smoothly to the beginning of a second verse.

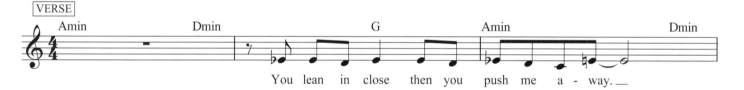

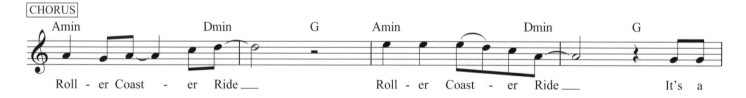

FIG. 1.4. "Roller Coaster Ride" Verse and Chorus

Listen again, and notice these new tools that *contrast* the two sections. The sections have different:

- numbers of phrases
- length phrases
- melodic rhythms and amount of space
- rhyme schemes
- pitches
- verse: blues melody; chorus: minor pentatonic melody
- types of counterpoint

WRITING EXERCISES

To practice using these tools, create a verse-chorus pair that contrasts, connects, and emphasizes the chorus as the emotional high point of the song. Use:

- a title chorus
- a standard verse with any of the standard rhyme schemes. Build intensity at the end of the verse by singing higher.

Trying using the chorus and verse you created in lessons 1 and 2. You may have to revise them to fit the guidelines we have been discussing.

Practice

Over this track, create an original verse-chorus pair.

7

Rewrite the Hits

Write an original verse-chorus pair over a loop from a hit song.

Write Your Own Song

Create an original two-measure or four-bar loop, and over it, write an original verse-chorus pair.

Challenge

Contrast sections by using a pentatonic scale in one section and a seven-note scale in the other.

Lesson 4. Bridge Over a Loop

Many verse-chorus songs also have a third contrasting section: a bridge. A bridge is created to keep the audience interested. In a loop song, you create a contrasting bridge over the same loop as the other sections.

Listen

Hit songs that have a bridge over a loop include:

- Selena Gomez: "The Heart Wants What It Wants"
- Katy Perry, feat. Snoop Dogg: "California Gurls"
- Maroon 5: "Girls Like You," "Sugar"

The bridge can include either a supporting lyric or summarize the main lyric idea or emotion. It usually:

- *contrasts* and *connects* with both surrounding sections
- *builds intensity* to the next section (usually the chorus, sometimes verse 3)

Listen to the bridge used in "Roller Coaster Ride," and notice that it features:

- intense, short phrases (1112)
- a rhyme scheme of aaax, which is surprising. The lack of rhyme feels a bit incomplete—perfect for setting up the next section. More on this in song 2.
- the development of the new rhythmic idea using the rhythm alone

STANDARD VS. SURPRISING RHYME SCHEMES

In rhyme scheme shorthand, the letters represent rhyme relationships of words at the end of lyric phrases. An x indicates words that do not rhyme.

Standard Rhyme Schemes	Surprising Variations
aaaa	aaax
aabb	aaax
abab	abaa, axax
xaxa	abaa, axax

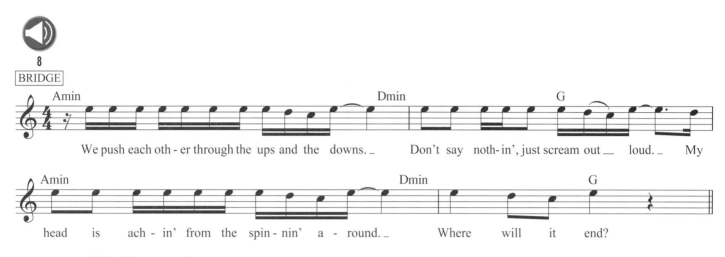

FIG. 1.5. "Roller Coaster Ride" Bridge

Listen to the "Roller Coaster Ride" verse, chorus, and bridge together. Notice how the bridge:

- connects with the other sections by using the same loop progression
- contrasts by using a new lyric structure, and a new melodic idea, with different notes, shapes, and rhythms

Roller Coaster Ride

Jimmy Kachulis

Medium Rock

You lean in close then you push me a-way. ＿   You're jump-in' out then you beg me to stay. ＿

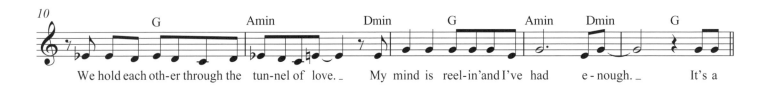

We hold each oth-er through the tun-nel of love. ＿   My mind is reel-in' and I've had e-nough. ＿   It's a

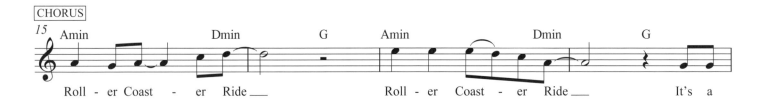

Roll - er Coast - er Ride ＿＿   Roll - er Coast - er Ride ＿＿   It's a

Roll - er Coast - er Ride ＿＿   Roll - er Coast - er Ride ＿＿

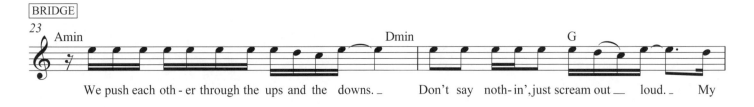

We push each oth-er through the ups and the downs. ＿   Don't say noth-in', just scream out ＿ loud. ＿   My

head is ach-in' from the spin-nin' a-round. ＿   Where will it end? (It's a)

FIG. 1.6. "Roller Coaster Ride" Full Song Form

Listen again to the three contrasting sections, and notice the intensity flow, and how they connect and contrast with each other.

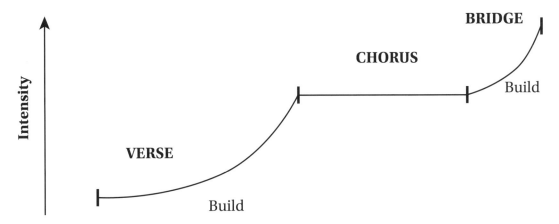

FIG. 1.7. Verse-Chorus-Bridge Song Intensity Flow

WRITING EXERCISES

In each of the following, try using the sections you created for lessons 1 and 2. To create a bridge, try using high notes, short rhythms, and short phrases.

10, 11

Practice

Over this loop, create an original bridge (melody and lyrics) that uses high notes, short rhythms, and short phrases. You can use the full song form track if you want to create a more complete song.

Rewrite the Hits

Take a loop from another song, and over it, create an original bridge that uses high notes, short rhythms, and short phrases.

Write Your Own Song

Over the loop you used in lessons 1, 2, and 3, create an original bridge that uses this lesson's tools to contrast, connect, and build intensity into the last chorus.

Challenge

Create a rap bridge with a melodic chorus, and see which one is most effective for your song.

COMPLETE FORM FOR VERSE-CHORUS WITH BRIDGE

To create a complete verse-chorus-bridge song, create a second lyric verse to the melody from verse 1. Insert the second verse into the form like this:

| Verse 1 | Chorus | Verse 2 | Chorus | Bridge | Chorus |

Verse-Chorus Variations ("Celebrity" Version 1)

In this next song, we will move beyond the simple verse-chorus loop song. Here, you'll see how to use different chord progressions to highlight ideas, connect sections, and build up intensity. You'll also learn how to create surprising verses and bridges that get off the loop and move around, before moving into the last chorus. As usual, you'll build each section and then learn how to connect and contrast them, building a complete song.

Lesson 5. More Standard Chorus Types

Some standard chorus types have *swing lines* (non-title lines) as well as title lines.

Listen to this chorus, and notice how the non-title swing lines:

- summarize the main emotion of the song in a new way
- don't rhyme
- are lyrically independent of each other

The four phrases are each two measures long (2222). We can diagram this chorus as:

T – T –

...with "T" representing the title and "–" representing the swing lines.

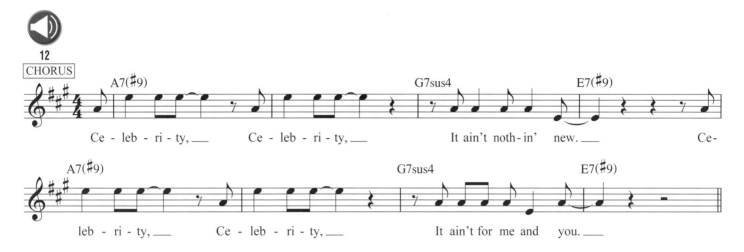

FIG. 2.1. "Celebrity" Chorus

Listen again, and notice how the title and swing lines:

- have contrasting pitches, rhythms, and shapes to help the title stand out
- have different chord progressions
- emphasize the title by repeating it exactly: lyric, melody, and harmony
- de-emphasize the swing lines, compared to the title, by repeating the music but with different lyrics
- use different progressions—a *great* way to contrast them

Using T to represent the title, a dash (–) to represent a swing line, P1 for progression 1, and P2 for progression 2, we can diagram it as:

Celebrity, Celebrity	P1	T
It ain't nothin' new	P2	–
Celebrity, Celebrity	P1	T
It ain't for me or you	P2	–

THE SEVEN STANDARD CHORUS TYPES

The title choruses in lesson 1 (TT and TTTT) are the first of seven standard chorus types. Here are all seven standard chorus types that use titles and swing lines, including the ones in this lesson, that you'll be using in the rest of this book:

TT

- Aretha Franklin: "Chain of Fools"
- The Beatles: "You've Got to Hide Your Love Away"
- Maroon 5: "She Will Be Loved"
- The Police: "Don't Stand So Close to Me"
- Marvin Gaye: "How Sweet It Is (To Be Loved by You)"

TTTT

- Rihanna: "Disturbia"
- Leonard Cohen: "Hallelujah"
- Bruce Springsteen: "Born in the USA"
- Marvin Gaye: "Let's Get It On"
- Bob Marley: "No Woman, No Cry"
- The Police: "Spirits in the Material World"
- Rihanna: "We Found Love"
- The Emotions: "Best of My Love"
- Bob Dylan: "Knockin' on Heaven's Door"

– T – T

- Sara Bareilles: "King of Anything"
- Cyndi Lauper: "Time after Time"
- David Guetta: "Titanium"
- Aerosmith: "I Don't Want to Miss a Thing"
- Selena Gomez: "A Year without Rain"
- Justin Bieber: "Love Yourself"
- David Guetta: "Without You"
- Maroon 5: "Animals," "One More Night"
- Taylor Swift: "Forever and Always"
- Bon Jovi: "Livin' on a Prayer"
- Smokey Robinson: "I Second That Emotion"
- Earth, Wind & Fire: "Boogie Wonderland"

T – T –

- Marvin Gaye: "I Heard It through the Grapevine"
- Mariah Carey: "Without You"
- The Beatles: "Drive My Car," "All My Loving," "I'm a Loser," "Can't Buy Me Love," "She Loves You"
- The Rolling Stones: "Brown Sugar"
- Tina Turner: "What's Love Got to Do with It"
- Melissa Etheridge: "Come to My Window"
- Selena Gomez: "Naturally"
- John Legend: "All of Me"
- Green Day: "21 Guns"
- Shawn Mendes: "Treat You Better"
- Earth, Wind & Fire: "After the Love Is Gone"
- The Four Tops: "Baby I Need Your Loving"
- Stevie Wonder: "I Just Called to Say I Love You"

T – – T

- Kesha: "Praying"
- Daughtry: "No Surprise"
- Kelly Clarkson: "A Moment Like This"
- Aaron Neville: "Everybody Plays the Fool"
- Michael Bolton: "How Can We Be Lovers"
- Kenny Rogers: "Lucille"
- Garth Brooks: "Ain't Going Down till the Sun Comes Up"

T – – –

- Roberta Flack/Donnie Hathaway: "The Closer I Get to You"
- The Beatles: "Rain"
- Jason Mraz: "I Won't Give Up"
- Sting: "Fortress around Your Heart"
- Maroon 5: "This Love"
- James Taylor: "Fire and Rain"
- Joni Mitchell: "Both Sides Now," "Urge for Going"
- Michael Jackson: "Man in the Mirror"

– – – T

- Kris Kristofferson: "Me and Bobby McGee"
- Bruce Springsteen: "Dancing in the Dark"
- Justin Bieber: "Mistletoe"
- Gary Morris: "Wind Beneath My Wings"
- The Police: "King of Pain"
- Green Day: "Holiday"
- Ed Sheeran: "Perfect"
- Smokey Robinson and the Miracles: "Tracks of My Tears"
- The Rolling Stones: "Jumpin' Jack Flash"
- Ed Sheeran: "Castle on the Hill"
- Rihanna: "Stay"
- Jason Mraz: "I'm Yours"
- Kelly Clarkson: "My Life Would Suck without You"
- Bruno Mars: "When I Was Your Man"
- Bob Dylan: "Like a Rolling Stone"

WRITING EXERCISES

Create a lyric title and three swing lines. When creating swing lines:

- Summarize the lyric theme in different ways.
- Make them lyrically independent.
- Make them a different length than the title.
- Rhyme is optional.

Then create lyrics to the five standard chorus types.

- Choose any of your new chorus types with swing lines.
- Use contrasting pitches, rhythms, and shapes, and chord progressions to contrast the title and swing lines.
- Use some tools to emphasize the title: long notes, space, melodic leaps.

13

Practice

Set this lyric or your original chorus lyric melodically over this track. Although any standard type will work, to connect your chorus to these two different progressions, try using either T–T– or –T–T.

Rewrite the Hits

Set an original chorus lyric melodically over the chords to a hit song that has two different progressions for the swing lines and titles.

Write Your Own Song

Set an original chorus lyric melodically over an original track that has two different progressions for the swing lines and titles.

Lesson 6. Surprising Verses

Musically, you may feel the need for more harmonic variety than using a loop. Here, you'll learn how to use a different variation of the loop-progression approach. You may also feel a song needs a more interesting verse than one of the simple standard verse types. We'll see a number of ways you can vary those standard verses that use a standard phrasing (2222) and rhyme scheme. These are ways to create *surprising verses*.

Listen

Hit songs that use surprising lyric moves include:

A Surprising Rhyme Scheme

- Hunter Hayes: "Wanted"
- The Beatles: "All You Need Is Love"
- Big Time Rush: "Til I Forget about You"
- Lorde: "Royals"
- Green Day: "21 Guns"
- Justin Bieber: "Sorry"
- Jason Mraz: "I Won't Give Up"

Added Phrases

- Daughtry: "Waiting for Superman"
- Hunter Hayes: "I Want Crazy," "Invisible"
- Taio Cruz: "Dynamite"
- Aretha Franklin: "Baby I Love You"
- The Four Tops: "Same Old Song," "Reach Out I'll Be There"
- Train: "50 Ways to Say Goodbye"
- Taylor Swift: "Fifteen"

Hit songs that build intensity melodically and/or harmonically include:

- Lorde: "Royals"
- Daughtry: "Battleships"
- John Legend: "All of Me"
- Taio Cruz: "Dynamite"
- Lady Gaga: "Applause," "I'll Never Love Again"
- Aretha Franklin: "Baby I Love You"
- Justin Bieber: "Sorry"
- Maroon 5: "She Will Be Loved"

- Bruno Mars: "Grenade"
- Hall & Oates: "She's Gone"
- The Beatles: "All You Need Is Love," "Drive My Car"
- Adele: "When We Were Young"
- Green Day: "21 Guns"
- Jason Mraz: "I Won't Give Up"
- Kelly Clarkson: "Because of You"
- Beyoncé: "I Was Here"

Listen to this surprising verse, and notice how it uses some of these lyrical and melodic tools:

- five phrases
- phrase lengths (in measures): 22221
- rhyme scheme: xaxaa
- development of the melodic idea by repeating the rhythm and changing the shape

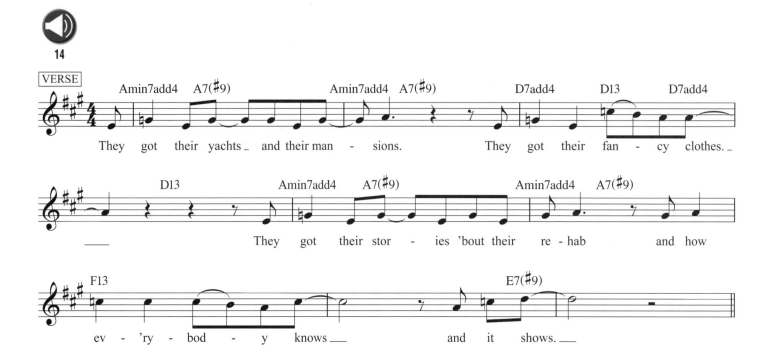

FIG. 2.2. "Celebrity" Verse

Listen again, and notice how it:

- varies a four-bar loop by adding a V chord at the end—a pitch variation

- varies the chorus progression from lesson 5 by changing the harmonic rhythm and adding a chord. Using a rhythm variation and/or a pitch variation are great ways to get more mileage out of a loop.

- builds intensity at the end into the coming chorus with: shorter phrases, faster rhymes, higher notes, an ending on the V chord, and then hanging onto it

VARIATIONS OF CHORD PROGRESSIONS

- *Rhythm variations* alter any progression using these tools condense it, expand it, change the order of chords, use an irregular chord rhythm.
- *Pitch variations* take any progression and: add a chord, subtract a chord, replace a chord, add a pedal part.

Here are some typical ways to create surprising verses:

- Use a surprising rhyme scheme in a four-line verse.

- Add a phrase to the end for a five-phrase verse. (Rhyming it is optional.)

- Use shorter phrases and/or higher notes at the end to build intensity.

- Hang onto the last chord a little longer to prolong the intensity.

WRITING EXERCISES

In the following, use at least one of the tools in this lesson to create a surprising verse.

Practice

15

Set this lyric or your original lyric using different melodic ideas over this track, repeating the rhythm and changing the shape. Build intensity at the end by using higher notes.

Rewrite the Hits

Set an original surprising lyric to a variation of a verse track from a hit song that has a V or ♭VII chord at the end.

Write Your Own Song

Set an original surprising lyric over an original progression that varies a loop by using the V or ♭VII chord at the end.

Lesson 7. More Contrast and Connection: Verse to Chorus

The principles of *connection* and *contrast* are essential with surprising verses as well.

Listen to this surprising verse and standard chorus, and notice the tools used to connect and contrast the verse and chorus, as in "Roller Coaster Ride":

- The end of the verse *builds* intensity and *connects* to the chorus.

- The verse *contrasts* melodically with the *more dramatic* chorus.

- There are different lengths of phrases, numbers of phrases, melodic rhythms, amounts of space, and rhyme schemes.

FIG. 2.3. "Celebrity" Verse and Chorus

Listen again, and notice the following new tools that contrast the two sections, and help the title stand out:

- One section is standard, one is surprising.

- Different harmonic rhythms (chord rhythms) and bass lines.

- The chorus uses a variation of the progression used in the verse.

WRITING EXERCISES

In combining any verse-chorus pairs below, try to:

- Contrast the sections lyrical, harmonically, and melodically.
- Use either a variation of the same progression, or a different loop.
- Build intensity at the end of the verse.
- Make the chorus feel like the emotional high point of the song.

Practice

Combine your "Practice" verse from lesson 6 with your "Practice" chorus from lesson 5. Consider how the tools discussed can help create contrast between the two sections, and possibly revise your song sections to make them more distinct. You can use the full song form track if you want to create a more complete song.

Rewrite the Hits

Combine your "Rewrite the Hits" examples from the previous lessons, consider the points in this lesson, and possibly revise the complete song to make sure that they connect to each other well.

Write Your Own Song

Combine your "Write Your Own Song" examples from the previous lesson, consider the points in this lesson, and possibly revise the complete to make sure that they connect to each other well.

Lesson 8. Moving Bridge

The next type of bridge is the *moving bridge*. Harmonically, it sort of "moves around" in the key, *often avoiding the I chord*. Although you're learning it in this song form, it can be used in *any* song form.

Listen

Hit songs that have a moving bridge include:

- The Beatles: "Ticket to Ride"
- Smokey Robinson and the Miracles: "Tracks of My Tears"
- Demi Lovato: "Skyscraper"
- Martha and the Vandellas: "Dancing in the Street"
- Sam and Dave: "Soul Man"
- Kesha: "Your Love Is My Drug"
- Selena Gomez: "Come and Get It," "Love You Like a Love Song"

- Taylor Swift: "Delicate"
- Luke Combs: "Beautiful Crazy"
- Kelly Clarkson: "Stronger"
- Justin Bieber: "One Less Lonely Girl"
- Lady Gaga: "I'll Never Love Again," "Born This Way"
- Beyoncé: "Best Thing I Never Had"
- Green Day: "21 Guns"
- Shawn Mendez: "Mercy"

Listen to the following moving bridge, and notice how it:

- uses a standard lyric rhyme scheme
- has three phrases
- builds intensity towards the end by using: a higher register, faster chord changes, an ascending bass line, and ends on the V chord

18

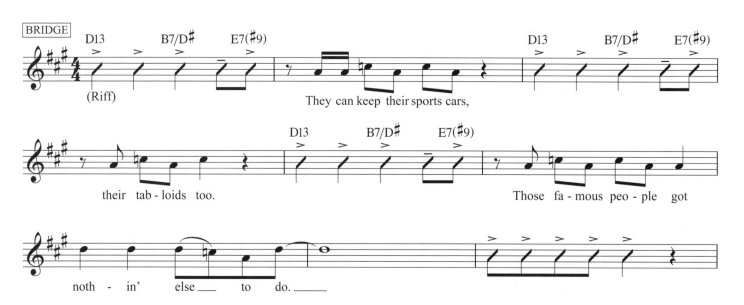

FIG. 2.4. "Celebrity" Moving Bridge

Listen again, and notice how it:

- begins on the IV chord (not the I chord) and ends on the V chord

- uses a variation of the IV V build progression by adding chords

- hangs onto the V after the vocal is finished, to build even more intensity

- uses the V of V chord (B7) from outside the key

- connects and contrasts with both the verse and the chorus by using: a different lyric structure, melodic idea, and different development tools than those used in the other song sections

The three sections have this intensity flow.

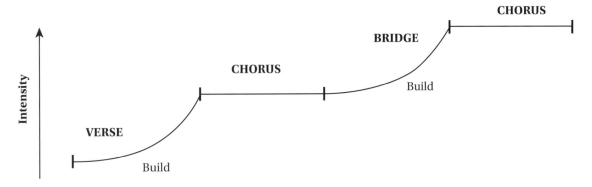

FIG. 2.5. Verse-Chorus Song Intensity Flow

Celebrity

Jimmy Kachulis

FIG. 2.6. "Celebrity" Full Song Form

BUILD PROGRESSIONS

A *build progression* (shown here in major) creates intensity. You can adapt them to any key color.

- V
- IV V
- IImin V
- IImin IIImin IV V

WRITING EXERCISES

Take your verse and chorus from lessons 5 and 6, and create a moving bridge that uses some of these tools:

- is in the same key
- begins on the chord that is not the I chord
- avoids big cadences to the I chord
- ends on an unresolved chord of tension, like V, ♭VII, IV, or IV minor
- uses chords outside the key
- uses a variation of one of the build progressions
- builds melodic intensity at the end of the bridge

Make sure it connects and contrasts with both the verse and the chorus

Practice

20, 21

Set this bridge lyric using different melodic ideas over track 20, repeating the rhythm and changing the melodic shape. Use track 21 if you want to create a complete song.

Rewrite the Hits

Choose a non-loop progression from a bridge of another song. Create an original bridge lyric and melody over that track.

Write Your Own Song

Take the verse-chorus pair from your original song in lesson 7. Create an original lyric and melody over your own variation of a build progression.

Challenge

To create a complete verse-chorus-bridge song, simply create a second lyric verse, and set it in this form:

| Verse 1 | Chorus | Verse 2 | Chorus | Bridge | Chorus |

Verse-Chorus with Cadences ("My Eleuthera")

In this next verse-chorus song, you will learn how to combine additional melodic and harmonic ideas to create even more varied verses and choruses. You'll see how to use special chord progressions called *cadences* to highlight ideas, connect sections, and build up intensity. As usual, you'll develop each section and then learn how to connect and contrast these new types, building a complete song.

Lesson 9. Choruses with Cadences

A *cadence* is a special kind of progression that sets up tension and forward motion towards the I chord of any key color. Cadences dramatically emphasize the lyric and create certain emotional effects. The most common cadences are:

CADENCE	PROGRESSIONS	EMOTION
Full	V or ♭VII to I	Resolved: singer is definite in their feelings
Plagal ("Amen")	IV to I IImin to I IV IIImin IImin to I	Resolved in a comforting way
Deceptive	V or ♭VII to any chord, except I (often VImin, IV, IVmin, VI major)	Ambivalent: singer has conflicting feelings
Half	Ends on V or ♭VII	Unresolved: singer is emotionally unresolved
Mixed	First chords borrowed from a parallel key: • ♭VII to I in major • IVmin to I in major	Mixed emotions: singer has two or more different emotions

In choruses, they're usually used in two ways:

1. **Cadence on the title only**. Avoid cadences on the swing lines.

Listen

Hit songs that have a cadence only on the title include:

- Sam Smith: "I'm Not the Only One"
- Aerosmith: "I Don't Want to Miss a Thing"
- Cyndi Lauper: "Time after Time"
- Green Day: "Time of Your Life"
- Gary Morris: "Wind Beneath My Wings"
- Rihanna: "Stay"
- Lady Gaga: "Born This Way"
- Hunter Hayes: "Somebody's Heartbreak"
- Sean Mendez: "Imagination"
- "You Will Be Found" from *Dear Evan Hansen*

It is most common in these standard chorus types, and it usually looks like this:

T‑T	Chorus Type:	–	T	–	T
	Progression:	P1	Cadence	P1	Cadence

T	Chorus Type:	–	–	–	T
	Progression:	P1	P1	P1	Cadence

T‑T	Chorus Type:	T	–	T	–
	Progression:	Cadence	P1	Cadence	P1

2. **Repeated cadences**. Here, *every phrase* has a cadence. You can *use this in any of the standard chorus types*—repeating either the same cadence, or different cadences.

Listen

Hit songs that use repeated cadences include:

- Sam Smith: "Stay with Me"
- Bruno Mars: "When I Was Your Man"
- Andy Grammer: "Fine by Me"
- Stevie Wonder: "I Just Called to Say I Love You"
- Marvin Gaye: "How Sweet It Is (To Be Loved by You)"
- Aaron Neville: "Everybody Plays the Fool"
- Phil Collins: "Easy Lover"
- Jess Glynne: "I'll Be There"
- Pharrell Williams: "Happy"
- Neil Young: "Rockin' in the Free World"
- Kelly Clarkson: "Since U Been Gone"
- Maroon 5: "This Love"
- Hunter Hayes: "Wanted"

Listen to this example, and notice how:

- the title and swing line ideas contrast melodically

- the title is set to a plagal cadence

- the chorus has the following lyric and harmonic structure:

You are My Eleuthr'a	T	cadence
You're callin' me, my tropical island home	–	contrasting progression
And deep inside Eleuthr'a	T	cadence
I'll carry you in my heart wherever I go	–	contrasting progression

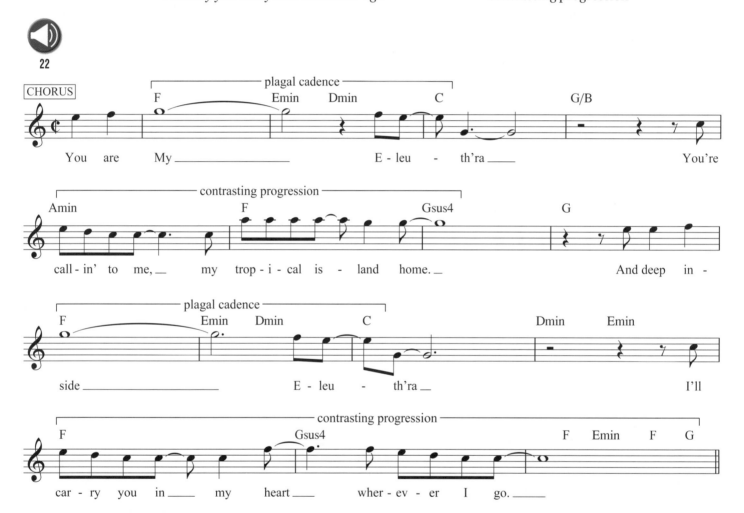

FIG. 3.1. "My Eleuthera" Chorus. Note that the chords outside the brackets are passing chords that connect the different progression types. There are also passing chords between the first and last chords of the cadences.

Listen again, and notice how:

- The cadences on the title emphasize it over the lyrics under the swing-line progressions.

- The plagal cadence emphasizes the resolved emotion in a comforting, reassuring way.

WRITING EXERCISES

In this writing exercise:

- Try setting your chorus lyric to both a series of repeated cadences and a setting that only has a cadence on the title. Which is a more effective way to present your lyric?

- Differentiate the swing lines and titles melodically as well as harmonically.

Practice

23

Set this lyric or an original lyric on an original melody, to this track, duplicating the structure of the "My Eleuthera" chorus melody.

Rewrite the Hits

Set an original standard chorus lyric to a two-progression chorus from a hit song. Duplicate that song's placement of title and swing lines.

Write Your Own Song

Set an original standard chorus lyric to an original progression that includes cadences.

Lesson 10. Two-Idea Verses

Combining different progressions and melodic ideas can give your verses more variety. The harmonic and melodic ideas are usually set up this way (P1 = progression 1, P2 = progression 2):

Harmony:	P1	P1	P1	P2
Melody:	Idea 1	Idea 1	Idea 1	Idea 2
Harmony:	P1	P2	P1	P2
Melody:	Idea 1	Idea 2	Idea 1	Idea 2

Listen

Hit songs that use two ideas in the verse include:

- Hall & Oates: "She's Gone"
- Green Day: "21 Guns"
- Tina Turner: "Private Dancer"
- The Temptations: "Ain't Too Proud to Beg"
- The Beatles: "All You Need Is Love," "Drive My Car"

This is especially effective in any kind of verse if P2 is a version on one of the build progressions (see lesson 8).

Listen to the following surprising verse, notice how it uses two progressions:

- P1 P1 P1 P2 (P2 is a variation on a build progression)
- five phrases over a standard sixteen-bar section
- the surprising xxxaa rhyme scheme
- two different melodic ideas

24

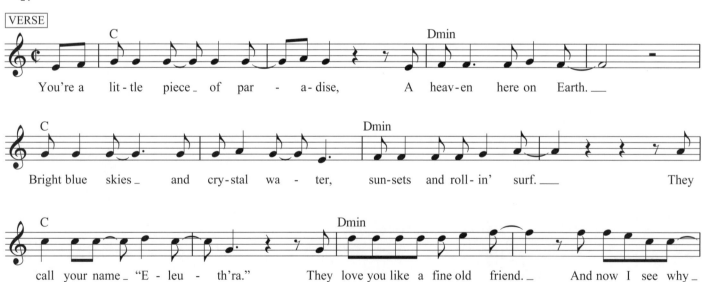

FIG. 3.2. "My Eleuthera" Verse

Listen again, and notice how the original melodic idea is sequenced higher in the last phrase—and how this builds melodic intensity. This combination of harmonic build and melodic build creates a lot of tension into the coming chorus.

WRITING EXERCISES

In each of these writing exercises, use one of these harmonic patterns:

- P1 P1 P1 P2
- P1 P2 P1 P2

  For P2, use a build progression and a higher melodic idea.

Practice

25

Set an original verse lyric on your own melody, over this track, duplicating the structure of the "My Eleuthera" verse.

Rewrite the Hits

Set an original verse lyric over a hit song's progression, and mirror its structure in your melodic ideas.

Write Your Own Song

Set an original verse lyric to two contrasting melodic ideas two contrasting chord progressions—coordinating the melodic and harmonic ideas.

Lesson 11. Cadences to Connect and Contrast Sections

In these more subtle verse-chorus songs, you also have many more ways to *contrast* and *connect* the sections.

The cadences you learned to emphasize titles are also effective ways to connect sections. When you end a verse away from the I chord—often V or ♭VII—you have two options for beginning the chorus:

- **Standard**: the chorus starts on the I chord. This uses a full cadence to connect the sections.

Listen

Hit songs that use a full cadence to connect the verse to the chorus include:

- Adele: "Remedy"
- Green Day: "21 Guns"
- Hunter Hayes: "Somebody's Heartbreak"
- Rihanna: "Take a Bow"
- The Beatles: "She Loves You," "You've Got to Hide Your Love Away"
- Boyz II Men: "I'll Make Love to You"
- The Temptations: "Ain't Too Proud to Beg"
- Lady Gaga: "The Edge of Glory"

- **Surprising**: the chorus starts on the chord that's not the I chord. This uses a deceptive cadence to connect the sections.

Listen

Hit songs that use a surprising cadence to connect the verse to the chorus include:

- Selena Gomez: "Hit the Lights"
- Train: "Hey Soul Sister"
- Jason Mraz: "I Won't Give Up"
- Kelly Clarkson: "Because of You"
- Hall & Oates: "She's Gone"
- The Beatles: "Drive My Car," "Ticket to Ride"
- Boston: "Amanda"

Listen to this verse-chorus pair, notice how cadences are used:

- verse ends with an unresolved half cadence on V (Gsus4)
- verse connects to the chorus with a deceptive cadence, moving from V to VI minor
- verse ends on a half cadence to G, which connects the chorus to the second verse

The audio begins with a short introduction.

My Eleuthera

Jimmy Kachulis

FIG. 3.3. "My Eleuthera" Full Song Form

Listen again, and notice how the sections contrast:

- **Melodically**: pitches, shapes, rhythms, standard/surprising types
- **Harmonically**: types of progressions, cadences, chords, where two progressions are used

Cadences help connect song sections, but the intensity flow is the same as all verse-chorus songs.

WRITING EXERCISES

For the following exercises, use:

- an unresolved half cadence at the end of the verse, and connect it to the chorus with either a full or deceptive cadence
- the other harmonic and melodic tools for contrast

27

Practice

Set this lyric or an original verse-chorus lyric on an original melody, over this track. Remember that this track begins with an eight-bar introduction before the verse.

Rewrite the Hits

Set an original verse-chorus lyric over a verse and chorus progression from a hit song. Duplicate its lyric structure.

Write Your Own Song

Set an original verse-chorus lyric over an original verse-chorus progression that uses cadences to connect the sections

Challenge

Write a full verse-chorus song with song sections connected using cadences, and include a moving bridge after the second chorus, like this:

Verse 1	Chorus 1	Verse 2	Chorus 2	Bridge	Chorus 3

Modulating Verse-Chorus ("Last a Lifetime")

In this verse-chorus song, you will learn a number of new skills, including how to:

- create *the most dramatic move of all*: change the key—called *modulation*—especially effective when you have two or more contrasting emotions—in the music and the lyric

- create surprising choruses based on the standard types you learned earlier

- create a bridge in a new key

As a result, you'll be able to create a song that can have as many as *three keys*—one in each section! As usual, you'll build each section and then learn how to connect and contrast them, building a complete song.

Lesson 12. Surprising Verse-Chorus and Modulating Verse-Chorus

For this song, you'll start with the verse and then learn all the aspects of changing key for the other sections. Surprising verses can be used in any song form.

Listen

Hit songs that use a surprising lyric structure include:

A Surprising Rhyme Scheme:

- Hunter Hayes: "Wanted"
- The Beatles: "All You Need Is Love"
- Big Time Rush: "Til I Forget about You"
- Lorde: "Royals"
- Green Day: "21 Guns"
- Justin Bieber: "Sorry"
- Jason Mraz: "I Won't Give Up"

Added Phrases:

- Daughtry: "Waiting for Superman"
- Hunter Hayes: "I Want Crazy," "Invisible"
- Taio Cruz: "Dynamite"
- Aretha Franklin: "Baby I Love You"
- The Four Tops: "Same Old Song," "Reach Out I'll Be There"
- Train: "50 Ways to Say Goodbye"
- Taylor Swift: "Fifteen," "You Belong with Me"
- Boyz II Men: "I'll Make Love to You"
- Stevie Wonder: "If You Really Love Me"

Hit songs that build intensity melodically and/or harmonically in the verse include:

- Daughtry: "Battleships"
- John Legend: "All of Me"
- Taio Cruz: "Dynamite"
- Lady Gaga: "Applause"
- Aretha Franklin: "Baby I Love You"
- Justin Bieber: "Sorry"
- Lady Gaga: "I'll Never Love Again"
- Maroon 5: "She Will Be Loved"
- Bruno Mars: "Grenade"
- Hall & Oates: "She's Gone"
- The Beatles: "All You Need Is Love"

Listen to this surprising verse, and notice the effects that you learned earlier, making this verse sound surprising:

- It's a four-bar loop that replaces a chord in bar 8 when it repeats (see figure 4.1).
- It builds intensity with: short phrases, faster rhymes, higher notes, and a build progression to an unresolved chord that connects to the chorus.

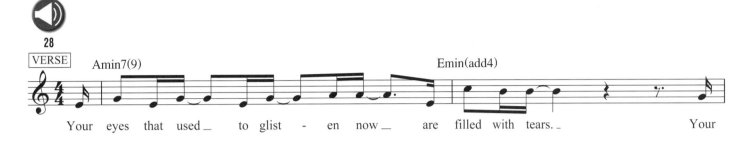

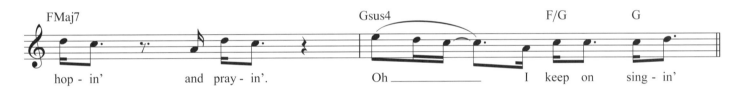

FIG. 4.1. "Last a Lifetime" Verse

Listen again, and notice that:

- The minor key expresses the sadness of a relationship that has gone wrong.
- It has a surprising five phrases over the eight bars (22211).
- It has a surprising rhyme scheme (axabb).

WRITING EXERCISES

Practice

29

Create a verse melody with sad lyrics over this track. This track begins with an introductory chord.

Rewrite the Hits

Create an original melody with lyrics over a hit song progression that expresses the feeling of that key color.

Write a Song

Create an original melody and lyrics over one of the song tracks from the previous lesson that expresses the feeling of that key color.

Lesson 13. Surprising Chorus: Lyrics

In preparation for creating a modulating verse-chorus song, you'll first learn how to create surprising choruses, lyrically.

Listen

Hit songs that use the following surprising structures include:

Three Phrases

- The Four Tops: "Ain't No Woman Like the One I've Got"
- John Mayer: "Your Body Is a Wonderland"
- Idina Menzel: "Defying Gravity"
- The Beatles: "Lucy in the Sky with Diamonds"
- Chuck Berry: "Maybellene"

Added Swing Lines

- James Taylor: "Sweet Baby James"
- Lee Brice: "I Drive Your Truck"
- Adele: "Someone Like You"
- Wynonna Judd: "I Saw the Light"
- Eric Clapton: "Lay Down Sally"
- Garth Brooks: "Friends in Low Places"
- Taylor Swift: "Gorgeous," "Begin Again"

Added Titles

- The Beatles: "Let It Be"
- Shawn Mendes: "In My Blood"
- Adele: "Turning Tables"
- Daughtry: "Battleships"
- Bon Jovi: "You Give Love a Bad Name"
- Taylor Swift: "Back to December," "22"

Replaced Titles

- The Beatles: "Ticket to Ride, "All You Need Is Love"
- Katy Perry: "Part of Me"
- Stevie Wonder: "I Ain't Gonna Stand for It"
- Selena Gomez: "Love You Like a Song"
- The Rolling Stones: "You Can't Always Get What You Want"
- Yes: "Owner of a Lonely Heart"
- Bonnie Raitt: "Let's Give Them Something to Talk About"
- The Righteous Brothers: "You've Lost That Loving Feeling"
- Bruce Springsteen: "Cover Me"
- Taylor Swift: "We Are Never Ever Getting Back Together"

Stacked Choruses, Standard + Standard

- Justin Bieber: "Baby"
- Lady Gaga: "Shallow"
- Maroon 5: "Girls Like You"
- Bruno Mars: "Just the Way You Are"
- Adele: "Set Fire to the Rain"
- Steve Winwood: "Back in the High Life"
- Katy Perry: "Firework"
- Hunter Hayes: "Somebody's Heartbreak"
- Taylor Swift: "Should've Said No"

Standard + Surprising

- Kesha: "Die Young"
- Lady Gaga: "The Edge of Glory"
- Jess Glynne: "I'll Be There"
- Taylor Swift: "Fifteen"

Combine Variation Tools

- The Beatles: "All You Need Is Love"
- Michael Bolton: "Time, Love, and Tenderness"
- "Waving through a Window" from *Dear Evan Hansen*
- Sara Bareilles: "Love Song"
- Kelly Clarkson: "Breakaway"
- Adele: "Water under the Bridge," "Rumour Has It"
- Hunter Hayes: "Invisible"
- Shawn Mendes: "In My Blood"
- Bon Jovi: "Blood on Blood"

Standard choruses can be effective. However, if you feel the need for a more surprising chorus, here are some tools you can use to create lyric structures for surprising choruses.

Lyrically, you can take a standard chorus and: subtract, add, or replace a phrase, stack any two types together, and combine any of these.

Most standard choruses use exact repetition when the title is repeated. In addition to the lyrical/melodic surprises discussed, you can also create a surprising chorus by musically varying a repeated title, changing the melody and/or harmony. These variation techniques are often used in this standard chorus type to add interest.

(Quotation marks around "T" represent a musically varied title.)

- Standard: T T T T
- Surprising: T "T" T "T"

Lastly, try combining any of these tools.

In the following table, each standard chorus type is followed by surprising options using the variation tools.

Surprising Chorus Lyrics

Tool	Standard Chorus	Surprising Variation
Subtract a swing line	– – – T	– – T
Subtract a title	T T T T	T T T
Add swing line(s)	T – – T	T – – – T
Add a title	– T – T	– T – T + T
Replace a title	T T T T	T T – T or T T T –
Stack *any* two types (some possibilities)	Standard + Standard	– T – T + – – – T
	Standard + Surprising	T – – T + T T – T

In the "Last a Lifetime" chorus, notice the surprising variations of the title. Notice how much variety you can get out of the same phrases.

- It has this structure: T – "T" – "T".

- It's a variation on the standard type T – T – that adds a title at the end.

- The lyric varies the repeated title.

Lovin' should Last a Lifetime	T
Forever is not just a word	–
Lovin' should Last a Lifetime for us	"T"
So let's fall in love all over again	–
And make it Last a Lifetime	"T"

WRITING EXERCISES

Practice

Create a five-line surprising chorus lyric.

Rewrite the Hits

Take any standard chorus from a hit song, and create surprising versions.

Write a Song

Write an original standard chorus, and then create a surprising version of it using any of the tools from this lesson.

Challenge

Stack two chorus types together. Some people hear this as a simple chorus and a "post-chorus."

Lesson 14. Modulation Types

The most dramatic contrasting move you can make in any song form is to change keys. This is called "modulation," and it usually accompanies a big change in the lyric's emotion. Always remember: *in order to be effective, changing keys has to be coupled with a change in the lyric emotions.*

In preparation for creating your modulating verse-chorus song, let's review the types of modulations.

EMOTIONS OF THE KEY COLORS

As discussed in the introduction, here are the five key colors with their general connected emotions:

KEY COLOR	Major	Mixolydian	Dorian	Minor
MAIN EMOTIONS	• Brightest • Happiest • Most optimistic	• Major type, but darker • More somber • Can be funky	• Minor type, but a little brighter • Also good for grooves	• Darkest • Most somber
Blues has its own combination of emotions, not as easily described.				

As you move to the right in the table, notice that the emotions get progressively emotionally darker, and to the left, progressively brighter. Keep these in mind when you decide to modulate. What change of emotions are you trying to express?

TYPES OF MODULATIONS

There are three common types of key relationships in modulations:

- **Parallel keys** have the same tonic note with a different key color. C major, C minor, C Mixolydian, C Dorian, C blues are parallel keys.

Listen

Hit songs that use parallel key modulation include:

- Pharrell Williams: "Happy"
- Hunter Hayes: "Storm Warning"
- The Eagles: "Heartache Tonight"
- Kenny Loggins: "I'm Alright"
- Creed: "In America"
- James Taylor: "Fire and Rain"
- The Beatles: "With a Little Help from My Friends," "Here, There, and Everywhere," "While My Guitar Gently Weeps"
- Jimi Hendrix: "Foxy Lady"

- **Relative keys** have the same pitches, but a different tonic note and hence, color. C major, A minor, D Dorian, G Mixolydian are relative keys.

Listen

Hit songs that use relative key modulation include:

- Neil Young: "Rockin' in the Free World"
- Train: "50 Ways to Say Goodbye"
- Daughtry: "Waiting for Superman"
- My Chemical Romance: "Sing"
- Billy Joel: "Goodnight Saigon"
- Lady Gaga: "Paparazzi"
- Maroon 5: "This Love"
- The Beatles: "Getting Better," "We Can Work It Out"
- The Police: "King of Pain," "Spirits in the Material World"
- Tina Turner: "Private Dancer"
- Bob Marley: "Could You Be Loved"
- Mr. Mister: "Kyrie"
- The Rolling Stones: "The Last Time"

- **Surprising keys** are characterized by either a surprising key color or tonic note. C major to E♭ major, or G minor, or E minor, etc. are surprising keys.

Listen

Hit songs that use a surprising key modulation include:

- Hairspray: "Without Love"
- Phil Collins: "Only You Know and I Know"
- Toni Braxton: "Unbreak My Heart"
- The Beatles: "Good Day Sunshine," "Something," "Lucy in the Sky with Diamonds"
- Eric Clapton: "Bell Bottom Blues"
- The Police: "Don't Stand So Close to Me," "Invisible Sun"
- The Rolling Stones: "Street Fighting Man"
- The Four Tops: "Baby I Need Your Loving"
- Stevie Wonder: "If You Really Love Me"

In "Last a Lifetime," you will learn how to modulate between parallel and relative keys in a verse-chorus song with a bridge.

HOW TO MODULATE

Modulation in and out of keys is very easy. There are a few common ways. The first three ways can be used for any of the modulation types.

1. **Stop-and-Start Modulation.** This is the easiest way to change key. Simply end the first section in the first key, then just start the next section by playing in the new key color!

Key	Verse				Chorus			
	C	Dmin	Emin	F	Amin	G	F	G
C Major	I	IImin	IIImin	IV				
A Minor					Imin	♭VII	♭VI	♭VII

2. **V Chord of the New Key.** Introduce the new key with its own V or ♭VII chord. For example:

Key	Verse				Chorus			
	C	Dmin	Emin	E7	Amin	G	F	G
C Major	I	IImin	IIImin					
A Minor				**V7**	Imin	♭VII	♭VI	♭VII

new
key

3. **Pivot Chord.** Find a chord that's in both keys to "pivot" between them. For example, a verse in A minor modulating to a chorus in C major both share the chord G, which is the ♭VII of A minor and the V of C major. In this case, G is the pivot chord between both keys:

Key	Verse				Chorus			
	Amin	G	F	**G**	C	Dmin	Emin	F
A Minor	Imin	♭VII	♭VI	**♭VII**				
C Major				**(V)**	I	IImin	IIImin	IV

pivot

4. **Deceptive Cadence.** The verse ends on a V chord or ♭VII chord and uses a deceptive cadence to go into a surprising key. This is really effective for surprising modulations. For example, modulating from C major to A major:

Key	Verse				Chorus			
	C	Emin	F	G	A	E/A	D/A	E/A
C Major	I	IIImin	IV	**V**	**VI**			
A Major					Imin	V/1	IV/1	V/1

deceptive
cadence

WRITING EXERCISES

Create chord progressions for verse-chorus pairs, using each of the following modulations:

1. **Start and Stop**. Create each section by repeating a two-measure loop four times:
   - a verse in C minor and a chorus in C major (parallel key modulation)
   - a verse in A minor and a chorus in C major (relative key modulation)
   - a verse in C major and a chorus in E♭ major (surprising key modulation)

2. **V Chord of the New Key**. Create a verse that starts in one key and ends on the V chord or ♭VII chord of the new chorus key. For example, create a verse in A minor that ends on the G chord (V of C major).

3. **Pivot Chord**. Choose a pair of relative keys (see appendix C) that share chords. Create a verse in one key and end it on a shared chord, and start a chorus in the new key on that shared. For example, create a verse in C major, end it on an E chord (V of A minor), and begin the chorus also on that E chord.

4. **Deceptive Cadence**. Create a verse that starts in one key and ends on the V chord or ♭VII chord. Instead of going to the chorus in that key, move to a surprising chord for the chorus key. For example, create a verse in C major, end it on the G chord, and then move to the A major chord for the chorus in the key of A major.

Challenge

Sketch out the emotions each key suggests to you and start to generate lyric ideas that reflect those emotions.

DECIDING TO MODULATE

Here, you'll look at ways to decide to modulate from the verse to the chorus in a modulating song. However, *you can make these decisions and moves in any song form.*

When you create a verse that expresses a certain emotion, to decide what to do next:

1. If you feel like keeping the main emotion the same, stay in the same key color.

2. If you feel like changing the emotion, choose a key color that most closely expresses that emotion.

For "Last a Lifetime," I decided that the song should move from the verse sadness to a chorus emotion that says "Love should last forever, so let's try to get back to where we first fell in love." The key color that expressed that hope to me was major, so I tried the three types of major modulations (parallel, relative, surprising) and decided that relative major had the best feeling.

The next choice is *how to get to the new key.* Any of the ways from the earlier lesson would work fine. For me, the G chord is in both keys, and to resolve it to C major is also a deceptive move, making it a smooth modulation.

Lesson 15. Surprising Chorus: Modulation

Listen to this chorus, and notice:

- It's in the new brighter C major key color.

- It expresses a more hopeful emotion.

30

FIG. 4.2. "Last a Lifetime" Chorus

Listen again, and notice:

- a surprising chorus of five lines (T–"T"–"T")

- varies the repeated title in lines 3 and 5

- uses three different chord progressions to bring out a mix of emotions

Your next choice is how to get back to the original key for verse 2. Again, any of the ways you learned will work here. I decided to use the same G chord, for the same reasons discussed in previous lessons.

Listen again, and notice how this chorus:

- builds intensity at the end, ending on an unresolved chord, to lead into a second verse or a bridge

- ends with a chord in another key

- ends on an unresolved chord, setting up a connection to another section—in this case, to modulate back to A minor for verse 2

Now listen to the verse and chorus together, and notice:

- the intensity flow both within and between the sections

- the connections and contrasts between sections

- the shift of emotions, reflected in the change of key

FIG. 4.3. "Last a Lifetime" Verse, Chorus

WRITING EXERCISES

Review the emotion and structure of your verse from lesson 12 and decide:

- which new emotion you want to express in the chorus
- which key color expresses that emotion
- which modulate type works best

Practice

32, 33

Create a surprising chorus, and set it over track 32, duplicating its structure. Use track 33 if you want to create a verse-chorus pair.

Rewrite the Hits

Create an original surprising chorus, and set it over a progression from the hit song, duplicating its structure.

Write a Song

Create an original surprising chorus, and set it to your original progression.

Lesson 16. New-Key Bridge

The other common place you can use modulation in a song is in the bridge, in this case, called a "new-key bridge." Use it when there's yet another emotion that can't be captured with the keys of the verse and the chorus. It can be used in any song form.

Listen

Hit songs with new-key bridges include:

- Whitney Houston: "Savin' All My Love for You"

- The Beatles: "I Should Have Known Better," "While My Guitar Gently Weeps," "Things We Said Today," "We Can Work It Out," "Something"

- Derek & the Dominos: "Bell Bottom Blues"

- Celine Dion: "Because You Loved Me"

- Billy Joel: "Longest Time," "She's Always a Woman," "New York State of Mind," "Just the Way You Are"

In the verse-chorus form, the keys will look like this:

Verse	Chorus	Bridge
Key 1	Key 2	Key 3

Listen to this bridge, and notice how it uses tools you learned in the moving bridge (see lesson 8). It uses the following, in *C minor*:

- the parallel key of C minor to reflect another emotion

- a build progression (IVmin Vmin ♭VIMaj7 ♭VII7)

- it ends on the ♭VII chord (B♭)

In "Last a Lifetime," there are three keys:

Verse	Chorus	Bridge
A minor	C major	C minor

FIG. 4.4. "Last a Lifetime" Bridge

Then, listen to this bridge with the following chorus, and notice the shorter phrases at the end help it to build melodically.

FIG. 4.5. "Last a Lifetime" Bridge, Chorus

Now, listen to the whole song and notice:

- It contrasts standard and surprising structures.

- All three sections contrast melodically, harmonically, and lyrically.

- The key changes reflect the changing emotions.

- The intensity flow is the same as all simple verse-chorus songs.

The audio track begins with a four-bar introduction.

Last a Lifetime

Jimmy Kachulis

36

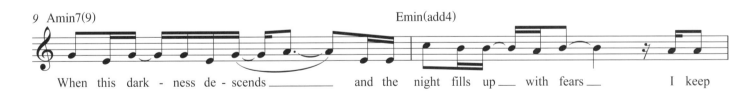

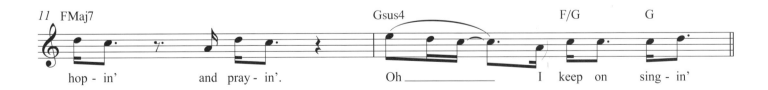

FIG. 4.6. "Last a Lifetime" Full Song Form

WRITING EXERCISES

In each of the following, try using any method for modulation, and refer to appendix B if you need to look up parallel and relative key relationships. Use your ears to explore surprising keys.

MODES

Try using modes as well as major and minor keys. These modes are relative: C Ionian (major), G Mixolydian, D Dorian, A Aeolian (minor). (See appendix A for references listing modes and scales.)

Practice

37, 38

Create a melody and lyric over track 37, and support the given modulation scheme with your own lyric story:

> **Verse**: A minor
> **Chorus**: C major
> **Bridge**: C minor

You can use track 38 if you want to create a more complete song. This audio track begins with a four-bar introduction.

Rewrite the Hits

Take a progression from a hit song, and create your own lyric and melody to reflect the original song's change of key colors and emotions.

Write a Song

Create a new verse-chorus song with a bridge, and set each section in a different key. Try using any of the key choices and ways to modulate we have discussed.

UNIT II.

PRECHORUS SONGS

SONG 5

Loop Prechorus Song ("It's You")

In this, the simplest of all prechorus song forms, the verse, prechorus, and chorus are all on the same loop. The loop prechorus song form is similar to the simple verse-chorus loop form, but with a prechorus between the verse and chorus.

Listen

Hit songs on a loop with a prechorus include:

- The Emotions: "Best of My Love"
- Earth, Wind & Fire: "Boogie Wonderland"
- Peter Gabriel: "Shaking the Tree"
- The Temptations: "Just My Imagination"
- Selena Gomez: "The Heart Wants What It Wants"
- Maroon 5: "Girls Like You," "Sugar," "Payphone"
- Kesha: "Die Young," "Tik Tok"
- Justin Bieber: "As Long as You Love Me"

- Demi Lovato: "Give Your Heart a Break"
- Ed Sheeran: "What Do I Know?"
- Nicki Minaj: "Fly"
- Daughtry: "Battleships"
- Lady Gaga: "Born This Way"
- Taylor Swift: "Red"
- Katy Perry: "Firework," "Teenage Dream," "Part of Me"
- Shawn Mendes: "Treat You Better," "Mercy," "In My Blood"

Note: The standard and surprising chorus and verse types you learned earlier are used in *all* the prechorus song forms.

Lesson 17. Verse in a Prechorus Song

Verses for prechorus songs are similar to those in simple verse-chorus songs. The big difference is that in prechorus songs, *the verse usually stays in the low register of the voice—often not building intensity at all. This static range in the verse is usually the reason why we feel the need for a prechorus.*

Listen to this example, and notice:

- The Mixolydian key color conveys singer's emotional struggle.

- The repetitive pedal part brings out a contemporary harmonic feel and keeps the Mixolydian key "grounded."

- There is a distinctive riff.

Here is the riff:

FIG. 5.1. "It's You" Riff

Here is the verse:

FIG. 5.2. "It's You" Verse

Listen again, and notice:

- The phrases stay in the low range over the two-bar loop.

- The voice sings for two measures and rests for two measures, letting the riff come through.

- The second melodic phrase varies the initial idea to keep it interesting.

WRITING EXERCISES

In each of the following, remember to stay in the low part of your range, and leave a lot of space, maintaining a low level of intensity.

Practice

Set an original verse lyric over this track.

Rewrite the Hits

Set an original verse lyric over a two- or four-measure loop from a hit song.

Write Your Own Song

Set an original verse lyric over a two- or four-measure original loop.

Lesson 18. Prechorus in a Loop Prechorus Song

Since verses in most prechorus songs don't build intensity, that becomes the job of the prechorus. The melodic tools you learned earlier to build intensity are the same in verse-chorus songs with a prechorus. Here, they're used for a whole prechorus section, *contrasting with the preceding verse.* When you write a prechorus, use:

- faster notes, shorter phrases, faster rhymes
- higher notes, ascending melodic shapes

Remember that since this is a loop prechorus song, *you only have melodic tools for building intensity and contrast,* since the loop is the same for all sections.

Listen to this example, and notice that in relation to the verse, this prechorus builds intensity by using: shorter phrases, faster rhymes, less space, and a higher register.

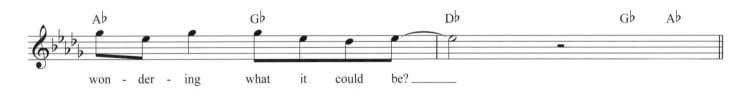

FIG. 5.3. "It's You" Verse, Prechorus

Listen again, and notice how this prechorus:

- uses those same melodic tools to contrast with the verse

- gets off the repetitive pedal part. Moving from a pedal part to a moving bass also builds the intensity.

PRECHORUS LYRICS

There are two approaches to prechorus lyrics:

- Continue the story of the preceding verse. In this case, prechoruses 1 and 2 would have *different* lyrics.

- Summarize the central idea, similar to a chorus. In this case, prechoruses 1 and 2 would have *the same* lyrics.

WRITING EXERCISES

In each of the following, create a prechorus that follows the loop verse you created in the previous lesson. Keep the loop the same or similar. Make sure it builds intensity melodically, and contrasts with that verse.

Practice

43

Set an original verse and prechorus lyric over this track.

Rewrite the Hits

Set an original verse and prechorus lyric over the two- or four-measure loop from the hit song you chose for the previous lesson.

Write Your Own Song

Set an original verse and prechorus lyric over the loop you created for your original song in the previous lesson.

Lesson 19. Chorus in a Prechorus Loop Song

Choruses for prechorus songs can be either standard or surprising. These choruses are still the emotional high point of the song, and as such, use the same tools for emphasis you learned earlier: high notes, long notes, repetition, space, and contrasting ideas for the title and swing line(s).

Remember that in the prechorus loop song, you only have melodic tools for emphasis and contrast.

Listen to this example of a surprising chorus (TTTT–), and notice how it uses those tools to dramatically emphasize the title, making the chorus sound like the emotional high point of the song:

- high notes, long note, exact repetition, contrasting ideas

- "out-of-sync" phrasing (beginning in the second bar of the loop and ending in the first bar) creating a "call-and-response" feeling between the voice and the riff

44

FIG. 5.4. "It's You" Chorus

VARYING THE LOOP

To add surprise, you can vary the loop by adding, subtracting, or replacing chords.

Now listen to the verse, prechorus, and chorus in order, and notice how the sections contrast and connect melodically and harmonically, and how the chorus is the emotional high point of the song.

It's You

Jimmy Kachulis

45

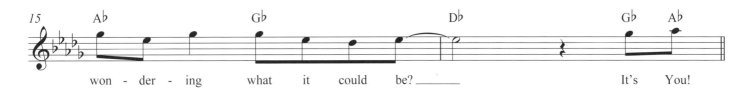

FIG. 5.5. "It's You" Full Song Form

Listen again, and notice this song's development of intensity levels.

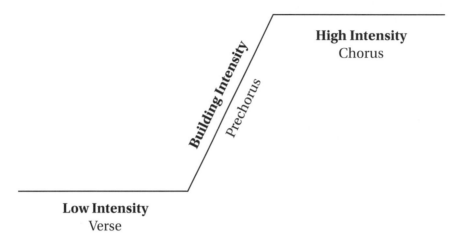

FIG. 5.6. Loop Prechorus Song Intensity Flow

WRITING EXERCISES

In each of the following, create either a standard or surprising chorus that contrasts with the verse and prechorus you created in the previous two lessons. Make sure your chorus sounds like the emotional high point of the song. Use the original loop or a similar version of it.

Practice

46, 47

Set an original chorus lyric over this track. You can use the full song form track if you want to create a more complete song.

Rewrite the Hits

Set an original chorus lyric over the loop from the hit song you chose in the previous two lessons.

Write Your Own Song

Set an original chorus lyric over the original loop you used in the previous two lessons.

Challenge

For a more complete song, create either loop bridge or moving bridge after the chorus. Make sure it contrasts with all the other three sections, and builds into a following chorus.

Write a full song by creating lyrics to a second verse, and if you like, a second prechorus, in this structure:

| Verse 1 | Prechorus 1 | Chorus 1 | Verse 2 | Prechorus 2 | Chorus 2 | Bridge | Chorus 3 |

Modified-Loop Prechorus Song ("Always the Last to Know")

Modified-loop prechorus songs have the loop in two of the three sections, and so have more variety than straight loop prechorus songs. In the most common version, the loop is in the verse and chorus, and there is a contrasting build progression in the prechorus. The prechorus also has a slightly different effect.

There are two ways to create this form:

1. Create the song in the order the audience hears it—the way you did in the loop prechorus form: verse, prechorus, chorus.

2. Create a simple verse-chorus, and if you feel the need for a prechorus, insert one between the verse and chorus.

    You'll practice the first approach in this section.

Listen

Hit songs in the modified loop form include:

- Queen: "Another One Bites the Dust"
- Julie Newton: "Angel of the Morning"
- Michael Jackson: "Billie Jean"
- Whitney Houston: "How Will I Know"
- Demi Lovato: "Skyscraper"
- Katy Perry, feat. Snoop Dogg: "California Gurls"
- John Mayer: "Your Body Is a Wonderland"
- Bruno Mars: "That's What I Like"
- Sean Mendes: "I Know What You Did Last Summer"
- Ed Sheeran: "Thinking Out Loud," "Castle on the Hill," "Barcelona"
- Toni Braxton: "Another Sad Love Song"

Lesson 20. Verse in a Modified-Loop Prechorus Song

The verse in a modified-loop prechorus song has the same characteristics as in the loop prechorus song: it stays low in intensity, allowing you to build intensity in the prechorus.

Listen to this example, and notice how:

- The two-bar loop riff is planted in the audience's ear before the vocal starts, acting as a sort of "instrumental hook."

- The verse melody stays in the low register, using a standard rhyme scheme (xaxa) and phrasing (2222).

Here's the riff:

FIG. 6.1. "Always the Last to Know" Riff

48

Here's the verse:

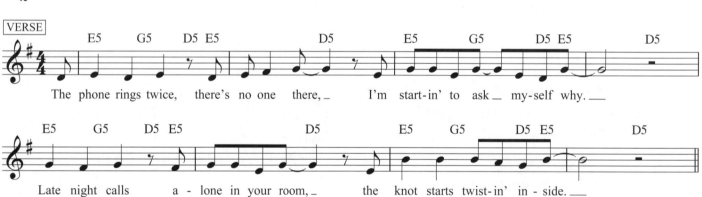

FIG. 6.2. "Always the Last to Know" Verse

Listen again, and notice how the idea in measures 2–3 of the verse is varied in measures 7–8 for more interest.

ADDING A HOOKY BASS

For something extra, try to create a melodic "hooky" bass under the verse loop. Then you'll be able to use the counterpoint tool you learned in song 1 in a new way.

WRITING EXERCISES

In each of the following, you can use either a loop or two-progression type of verse. Remember to keep the voice part low.

49

Practice

Set an original verse lyric over this track.

Rewrite the Hits

Set an original verse lyric over a track from a hit song that uses a modified loop.

Write Your Own Song

Set an original verse lyric over an original progression: either a loop or a two-progression verse.

Lesson 21. Prechorus in a Modified-Loop Prechorus Song

The prechorus in the modified-loop prechorus song often uses some of the same tools that build intensity in a moving bridge (see lesson 8).

Listen to this prechorus, and notice how it:

- builds intensity harmonically by using the progression: IVmin Vmin ♭VI V7(♯9)

- uses higher notes and continues to the highest notes

- has five bars

- hangs onto the V chord at the end, to build even more tension

50

FIG. 6.3. "Always the Last to Know" Prechorus

Now listen to the verse and prechorus, and notice how in the prechorus, *while the melodic tools build intensity, the rate of chord changes slows down*. This is a subtle decrease in intensity that eventually builds towards the end. These slower chord changes also contrast nicely with the verse.

FIG. 6.4. "Always the Last to Know" Verse, Prechorus

TIPS FOR WRITING PRECHORUSES

Similar to a moving bridge, some simple tips to create a prechorus in a modified-loop song include:

- Avoid the I chord.
- End on any unresolved chord.
- Connect and contrast it with the preceding verse.

WRITING EXERCISES

In all of the following, try slowing down the rate of chord change before you build up at the end.

Practice

Set an original prechorus lyric over track 52. Remember to keep it short—just five bars. You can also create a verse-prechorus pair over track 53.

Rewrite the Hits

Set an original prechorus lyric over a track that uses a build progression from the hit song you chose for your verse in the previous lesson.

Write Your Own Song

Set an original prechorus lyric over an original track. Use a build progression that contrasts and connects with the verse you created in the previous lesson.

Lesson 22. Chorus in a Modified-Loop Prechorus Song

The chorus in a modified-loop prechorus song is very similar to those used in the simple-loop version. The chorus is the emotional high point of the song, and connects and contrasts with the preceding verse and prechorus. You can use either standard or surprising chorus types.

Listen to this chorus, and notice it is:

- a surprising chorus (TT–T)

- in parallel counterpoint with the riff—in this case, parallel octaves, which are the exact same notes as the riff

54

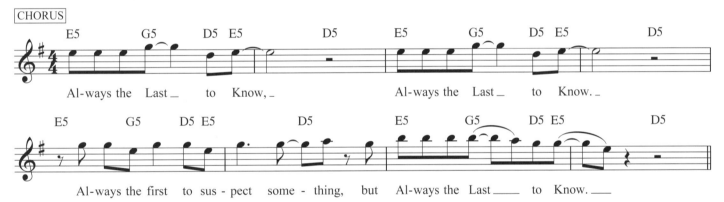

FIG. 6.5. "Always the Last to Know" Chorus

Now listen to the full verse, prechorus, and chorus, and notice:

- Each section contrasts and connects with the others.

- The slower chords in the prechorus decrease the intensity subtly, while the melody builds intensity.

Always the Last to Know

Jimmy Kachulis

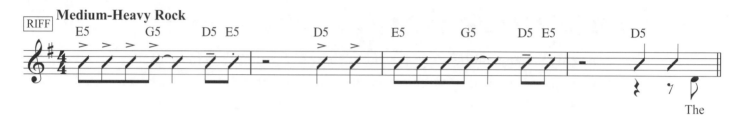

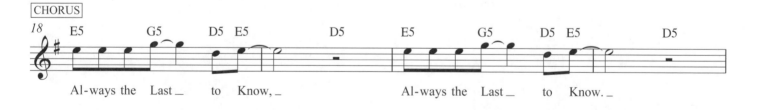

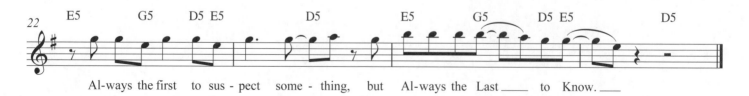

FIG. 6.6. "Always the Last to Know" Full Song Form

Listen again, and notice how singing parallel counterpoint in the chorus emphasizes the title and sounds like the emotional high point.

The flow of intensity can be diagrammed as follows:

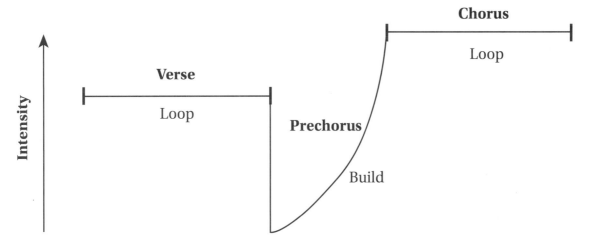

FIG. 6.7. Modified-Loop Song Intensity Flow

WRITING EXERCISES

In any of the following:

- Use any chorus type.
- Use the same loop you used in the verse lesson.
- Contrast and connect the chorus with the preceding verse and prechorus you already created.

Practice

56, 57

Set an original chorus lyric over this track. It is eight bars long. You can use the full song form track if you want to create a more complete song.

Rewrite the Hits

Set an original chorus lyric over the chorus progression from the hit song you used in the previous lesson.

Write Your Own Song

Set an original chorus lyric over the loop you created in the verse lesson.

Challenge

For a complete song, create either loop bridge or moving bridge after the chorus. Make sure it contrasts with all the other three sections, and builds into a following chorus.

Write a full song by creating lyrics to a second verse, and if you like, a second prechorus, in this structure:

| Verse 1 | Prechorus 1 | Chorus 1 | Verse 2 | Prechorus 2 | Chorus 2 | Bridge | Chorus 3 |

NEW TYPES OF MODIFIED-LOOP SONGS

There are a few newer types of modified-loop songs that are starting to emerge. Notice how they often start as loop-prechorus songs and then make some surprising moves.

- **Verse and Chorus-Loop/Chorus Non-Loop**. This type starts off like a loop song, and then uses any type of progression for the chorus.

Verse	Prechorus	Chorus
Loop 1	Loop 1	Any Progression

Hit songs in this form include:

- John Legend: "Love Me Now"
- The Fray: "How to Save a Life"
- Adele: "Water under the Bridge," "Rumour Has It"
- Shawn Mendes: "Imagination"
- Selena Gomez: "Me & the Rhythm"
- Ed Sheeran: "Perfect"

- **Verse Loop 1/Prechorus and Chorus Loop 2**. This type also starts off like a loop song. It then goes to another loop in the prechorus and stays there for the chorus.

Verse	Prechorus	Chorus
Loop 1	Loop 2	Loop 2

Hit songs in this form include:

- Lorde: "Royals"
- Daughtry: "No Surprise"

SONG 7

Classic Prechorus Song ("The Road Remains the Same")

In this classic version of the prechorus song, each section has a different progression. The flow of intensity is the same as the loop prechorus song: it starts low, builds in the prechorus, and hits home in the chorus. The difference is that the intensity shape is spread over a longer time. You can use standard or surprising moves is any sections.

Listen

Hit songs within the classic prechorus form include:

- Mariah Carey: "Emotions"
- Martha and the Vandellas: "Heatwave"
- Marvin Gaye: "I Heard It through the Grapevine," "How Sweet It Is (To Be Loved by You)"
- Stevie Wonder: "I Wish"
- Michael Jackson: "Man in the Mirror"
- Tina Turner: "What's Love Got to Do with It?"
- Bon Jovi: "You Give Love a Bad Name," "Livin' on a Prayer"
- Maroon 5: "Daylight"
- Bruno Mars: "Grenade," "When I Was Your Man"
- Green Day: "Good Riddance (Time of Your Life)"
- Taylor Swift: "Back to December"
- Adele: "Someone Like You," "Rolling in the Deep," "Set Fire to the Rain"
- Huey Lewis and the News: "If This Is It"
- Shawn Mendes: "There's Nothing Holding Me Back," "If I Can't Have You"
- "Waving through a Window" from *Dear Evan Hansen*
- Beyoncé: "Best Thing I Never Had"
- Bonnie Raitt: "Let's Give Them Something to Talk About"
- Melissa Etheridge: "Come to My Window"
- Gary Morris: "Wind Beneath My Wings"
- Aretha Franklin: "(You Make Me Feel Like A) Natural Woman"
- Jefferson Starship: "We Built This City"
- Bob Dylan: "Like a Rolling Stone"
- Billy Joel: "You May Be Right"

Lesson 23. Verse in a Classic Prechorus Song

Listen to this verse, and notice how it:

- stays in the low register

- uses a two-bar loop

- has a distinctive pedal part

58

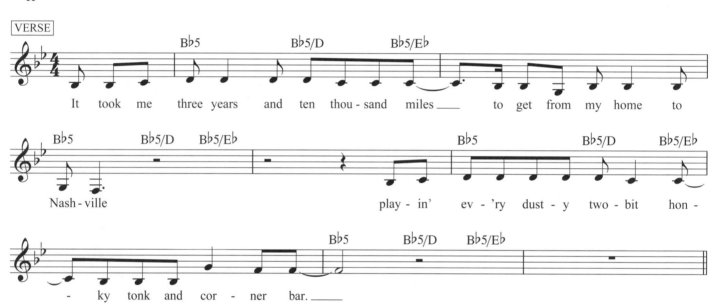

FIG. 7.1. "The Road Remains the Same" Verse

Listen again, and notice how it uses:

- four-bar phrases with lots of space that lets the pedal part come through

- a surprising rhyme scheme (xx)

All of these help the verse stay at a low intensity level and will give the song room to grow in the next two sections.

WRITING EXERCISES

In each of the following:

- Use either a standard or surprising verse.
- Follow the guidelines to keep the intensity low.

Practice

59

Set an original verse lyric over this track, following the guidelines for keeping the intensity low. The track begins with an introductory pickup measure.

Rewrite the Hits

Set an original verse lyric over a hit song that has either loop progression or a two-progression verse.

Write Your Own Song

Set an original verse lyric over a loop progression or a two-progression verse.

Lesson 24. Prechorus in a Classic Prechorus Song

The prechorus in the classic prechorus song has the same effect as the one in the loop song: it builds melodic intensity into the coming chorus. The difference is that it uses a build progression to also increase harmonic tension.

Listen to this prechorus, and notice how:

- It avoids the I chord (B♭) and starts on a new chord (G minor).

- It uses a surprising phrasing (244) and rhyme scheme (aax).

- The last line (ending on the long ā sound in "say") isn't rhymed.

- The build progression (IImin IIImin IV V) creates intensity at the end.

- It ends on the V chord (F).

60

FIG. 7.2. "The Road Remains the Same" Prechorus

Now listen to the verse and prechorus together, and notice how the prechorus:

- builds intensity using: shorter phrases, faster rhymes, higher notes, faster chord rhythms at the end, and ends on the V chord

- contrasts the verse's phrase lengths, number of phrases, rhymes, rhyme scheme, and whether it includes/omits the pedal part

61

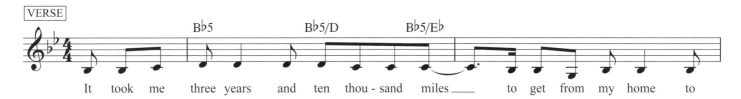

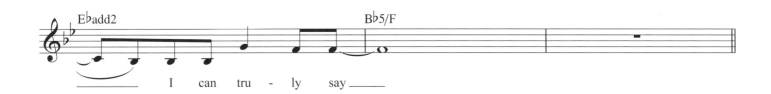

FIG. 7.3. "The Road Remains the Same" Verse, Prechorus

WRITING EXERCISES

In each of the following, remember to contrast the prechorus with the verse you created in the preceding lesson, and build intensity into the coming chorus.

Practice

62, 63

Set an original prechorus lyric over track 62 or a verse-prechorus pair over track 63.

Rewrite the Hits

Set an original prechorus lyric over a prechorus track you choose from a hit song (such as the one selected in the previous lesson).

Write Your Own Song

Set an original prechorus lyric over an original prechorus track, after the verse from the previous song.

Lesson 25. Chorus in a Classic Prechorus Song

The chorus in the classic prechorus song has the same effect as all the other standard and surprising choruses you learned so far. It contrasts and connects with the other sections and feels like the emotional high point of the song. However, it uses a different progression (or progressions) than either the verse or the prechorus.

Listen to this chorus, and notice:

- It is a surprising structure (TT–T).

- The last title is varied musically and overlaps with the beginning of the verse loop.

FIG. 7.4. "The Road Remains the Same" Chorus

Listen to the verse, prechorus, and chorus together, and notice:

- The sections melodically connect and contrast.

- The prechorus goes into the chorus with a deceptive cadence to the IV chord.

- The chorus feels like the emotional high point of the song.

- The chorus uses a different pedal part than the other sections, for contrast.

The Road Remains the Same

Jimmy Kachulis and
Shane Adams

FIG. 7.5. "The Road Remains the Same" Full Song Form

Now listen again, and notice the flow of intensity

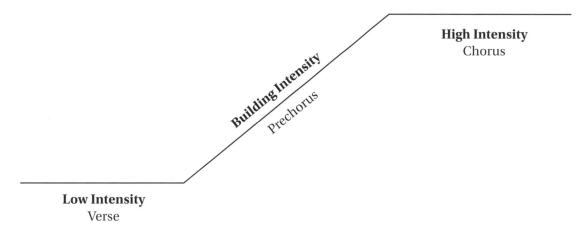

FIG. 7.6. Classic Prechorus Song Intensity Flow

WRITING EXERCISES

In each of the following, remember to use contrasting progressions and melodic ideas that start low. Build intensity from the verse through the prechorus into the chorus.

Practice

66, 67

Set an original chorus lyric over this track to follow the verse and prechorus you created in the previous two lessons. You can use the full song form track if you want to create a more complete song.

Rewrite the Hits

Set an original chorus lyric over a track from a hit song to follow the verse and prechorus you created in the previous two lessons.

Write Your Own Song

Set an original chorus lyric over your original track to follow the verse and prechorus you created in the previous two lessons.

SONG 8

Modulating Prechorus Song ("It's a Miracle")

This last type of prechorus song is the most challenging, and yet it can be the most dramatic. It uses the tools you learned in the modulating verse-chorus on a larger canvas.

Listen

Hit songs with modulating prechoruses include the following. Note: the verse, chorus, prechorus, and modulation types you learned earlier are used here as well.

- Foreigner: "I Want to Know What Love Is"
- Hall & Oates: "I Can't Go for That (No Can Do)"
- Maroon 5: "It Was Always You," "She Will Be Loved"
- Hunter Hayes: "Storm Warning"
- Bon Jovi: "You Give Love a Bad Name"
- Bob Marley: "Could You Be Loved"
- Marvin Gaye: "How Sweet It Is (To Be Loved by You)"
- Toni Braxton: "Unbreak My Heart"
- Bruno Mars: "Locked Out of Heaven"
- John Legend: "Love Me Now"
- Rihanna: "Stay"
- My Chemical Romance: "Sing"

Lesson 26. Verse in a Modulating Prechorus Song

Like the other prechorus examples, the verse in this type gives the subsequent sections room to build into the chorus.

Listen to this verse, and notice how it:

- stays in a lower register
- uses a four-bar loop, ending on the V chord

68

FIG. 8.1. "It's a Miracle" Verse

Listen again, and notice how it uses:

- a surprising phrasing (22112) and rhyme scheme (xaxxa)
- one- and two-bar phrases over the four-bar loop

WRITING EXERCISES

In each of the following:

- Choose either a standard or surprising verse based on what works best in your lyric story.

- Keep the intensity low, using the various tools we have discussed.

Practice

69

Set an original verse lyric over this track, following the guidelines for keeping the intensity low.

Rewrite the Hits

Set an original verse lyric over a hit song that has either loop progression or a two-progression verse.

Write Your Own Song

Set an original verse lyric over a loop progression or a two-progression verse.

Lesson 27. Prechorus in a Modulating Prechorus Song

The prechorus in a modulating prechorus song has the same effect as in a classic prechorus song: it builds intensity harmonically and melodically into the coming chorus. The big difference in a modulating prechorus song is that *it either starts to change key, or is already in a different key.* (See "Deciding to Modulate" in lesson 14 to decide which key color your song will move to.) You can use any of the keys and ways to modulate you learned earlier. It should also reflect any changes in the lyrical emotions.

Listen to this prechorus, and notice how it:

- starts on the IV chord (D minor)

- starts with a pedal in the bass to create tension

- has two phrases (a two-bar and a three-bar phrase) rhymed (aa)

- is a surprising five-bar section

- reflects a more exciting expectant lyrical emotion

- has an ascending bass line at the end for more tension

70

FIG. 8.2. "It's a Miracle" Prechorus

Now listen to the verse and prechorus together, and notice how the prechorus connects and contrasts with the verse. It:

- starts deceptively from the V chord to the IVmin chord (D minor)

- contrasts the phrase lengths, number of phrases, rhymes, rhyme scheme

- builds intensity towards the end with the ascending phrase, avoiding the I chord, and then ending on the V chord

FIG. 8.3. "It's a Miracle" Verse, Prechorus

The big difference here is the key. Here are some ways to hear this harmonic move:

- The D minor chord, with the pedal, starts to sound like D Dorian (the related key of A minor).

- The ending chord (G major) is the IV chord in D Dorian (see appendix A).

- The G chord is also the V chord of the chorus key (C major).

The modulation scheme looks like this:

Verse	Prechorus
A minor	D Dorian (related key)
ends on V chord (Esus4)	• deceptive cadence to D minor chord • ends on G chord

WRITING EXERCISES

In each of the following:

- Use a progression in a related key or a build progression in a parallel key.

- Contrast the prechorus with the verse you created in the preceding lesson.

- Use the tools we have discussed to build intensity into the coming chorus.

Practice

72, 73

Set an original prechorus lyric over this track.

Rewrite the Hits

Set an original prechorus lyric over a prechorus progression from a hit song.

Write Your Own Song

Set an original prechorus lyric over an original prechorus progression, to follow your verse from the previous lesson.

Lesson 28. Chorus and Full Song Form in a Modulating Prechorus Song

The chorus in the modulation prechorus song has the same effect as all the other standard and surprising choruses you learned so far. It contrasts and connects with the other sections, and feels like the emotional high point of the song. It uses yet a different progression, or progressions, than either the verse or the prechorus. *The big difference here is that it's in another key.*

Listen to this chorus, and notice:

- a surprising structure (TT–T)

- the repeated cadences

- the melodic cadence to "Do" (C natural) at the end

- the repeated titles set to varying music

74

FIG. 8.4. "It's a Miracle" Chorus

Now listen to the verse, prechorus, and chorus, and notice:

- The prechorus moves into the chorus with a deceptive cadence to the IV chord in the new key.

- The sections contrast in phrase lengths, number of phrases, rhymes, rhyme scheme, melodic shape, pitches, and register.

- The cadences connect the sections.

- The chorus feels like the emotional high point of the song.

It's a Miracle

Jimmy Kachulis

FIG. 8.5. "It's a Miracle" Full Song Form

The overall intensity flow is the same as the loop version:

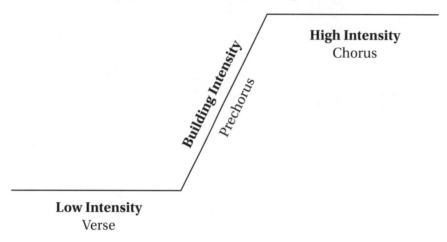

FIG. 8.6. Modulating Prechorus Song Intensity Flow

The modulation/cadence scheme looks like this:

Verse	Prechorus	Chorus
A minor	D Dorian (related key)	C major (related key)
• ends on V chord (Esus4)	• deceptive cadence to D minor chord • ends on G chord	• deceptive cadence to F chord: IV in C major

Listen again, and notice how the changing keys in each section reflect the changing emotions of the lyrics.

WRITING EXERCISES

In each of the following:

- Use contrasting progressions and melodic ideas that start low and build intensity from the verse to the chorus.

- Choose key colors that reflect any change in lyric emotions. Use any type of modulation.

76, 77

Practice

Set an original chorus lyric over this track to follow the verse and prechorus you created in the previous two lessons. You can use the full song form track if you want to create a more complete song.

Rewrite the Hits

Set an original chorus lyric over a track from a hit song to follow the verse and prechorus you created in the previous two lessons.

Write Your Own Song

Set an original chorus lyric over your original track to follow the verse and prechorus you created in the previous two lessons.

Unit III.

Verse/Refrain Songs

In this unit, you'll learn various approaches to the subtlest song form: the verse/refrain. It is the oldest of the current forms and has the following characteristics. It usually:

- has the title, or refrain line, *in the verse*
- has no chorus
- is in a slow or medium tempo
- has lyric content with a universal appeal across styles and genres

Although its traditional version doesn't occur often in very commercial songwriting, it has some distinct advantages:

- It is the most "covered," or rerecorded, song form. These classics seem to have a "life" after the original recording.
- You can use more sophisticated melodic and rhythmic ideas, since the audience doesn't have to sing along.

In addition, in unit IV, you'll learn how to combine it with the other forms to make it very, very commercial.

Standard Verse/Refrain ("Shelter Me from the Storm")

In this, the simplest of the verse/refrain types, you'll learn how to adapt the fundamental concepts you learned earlier to this song form.

Listen

Hit songs in a standard verse/refrain form include:

- Bruce Springsteen: "I'm on Fire"
- George Benson: "This Masquerade"
- Will Smith: "Fresh Prince of Bel-Air"
- Muddy Waters: "I Just Want to Make Love to You"
- Green Day: "Wake Me Up (When September Ends)"
- Hunter Hayes: "Everybody's Got Somebody But Me"
- The Script: "Breakeven"
- Sheryl Crow: "Strong Enough"
- Bob Dylan: "Blowin' in the Wind"
- Kelly Clarkson: "Breakaway" (verse 2)
- Johnny Cash: "I Walk the Line
- Kris Kristofferson "Help Me Make It Through the Night"

Lesson 29. Standard Verse/Refrain

In a standard verse/refrain form, the verse has the title, or "refrain line" of the song, embedded in it.

The title is usually in one of three places:

1. the first line (the least common)

2. the last line (the most common)

3. throughout the verse

LISTEN: REFRAIN LOCATIONS

First Phrase	Last Phrase	Throughout
• James Brown: "I Got You (I Feel Good)" • Beyoncé: "If I Were a Boy" • Jimi Hendrix: "Purple Haze" • The Beatles: "Michelle," "Something" • Huey Lewis: "I Want a New Drug" • Billy Joel: "Uptown Girl" • Harold Arlen and Yip Harburg: "Over the Rainbow"	• Adele: "Make You Feel My Love" • Green Day: "Wake Me Up When September Ends" • Justin Bieber: "U Smile" • Muddy Waters: "I Just Want to Make Love to You" • Billy Joel: "Just the Way You Are" • The Beatles: "I Feel Fine" • Simon and Garfunkel: "Sound of Silence" • Kris Kristofferson: "Help Me Make It Through the Night"	• Eric Clapton: "After Midnight" • Adele: "Hello" • Wilson Pickett: "In the Midnight Hour" • Stevie Wonder: "Part-Time Lover" • Sting: "Be Still My Beating Heart" • The Beatles: "Yesterday" • Taylor Swift: "Today Was a Fairytale" • Willie Nelson: "Crazy"

In this lesson, you'll learn the tools for setting up the first, most common, version: the refrain line at the end. The intensity flow in this form is subtler than the others discussed; the development happens *within the one section*. The standard four-phrase version looks like this:

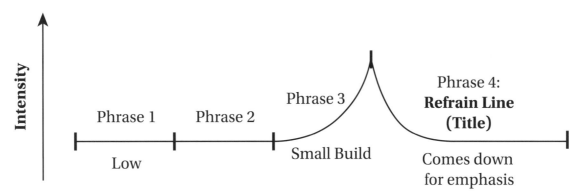

FIG. 9.1. Verse/Refrain Intensity Flow

Listen to this example, and notice how the verse:

- begins in the low register

- builds melodically in phrases 2 and 3

- builds harmonically in phrase 3 by getting off the pedal and moving away from the I chord to the IV chord

- comes down in intensity in the title phrase (i.e., refrain)

- has an "instrumental hook" up front, which helps the audience remember the song

- includes the title that overlaps with the beginning of the "instrumental hook"

Shelter Me from the Storm

Jimmy Kachulis and
Jon Aldrich

FIG. 9.2. "Shelter Me from the Storm" Full Song Form

Listen again, and notice how the end-line title (refrain) is emphasized:

- *melodically*, with unique notes, shape, rhythms, and a melodic cadence to the Do of the key. It also uses *internal repetition*—breaking up the title before eventually completing it. This particular example also uses a note outside the key (A♭).

- *harmonically*, with unique chords, and a full cadence to the I chord of the key

VERSE/REFRAIN RHYME SCHEMES

In a four-line verse/refrain, you can use a:

- standard rhyme scheme: aaaa (aabb) or abab (xaxa)

- surprising rhyme scheme: aaax or abaa

Here are two easy ways to set up the harmony for a standard verse/refrain:

	Phrase 1	**Phrase 2**	**Phrase 3**	**Phrase 4**
Repeated I Chord:	I chord	I chord	I chord	Cadence
Repeated Progression:	P1	P1	P1	Cadence

FIG. 9.3. Verse/Refrain Progression Structure

WRITING EXERCISES

In each of the following, create:

- a verse that uses sensory images to show the song's emotion and meaning

- a title that summarizes the main idea and emotion of the lyric

Also, use the tools you learned to build intensity towards the title, and then emphasize it.

Practice

Set an original four-line verse/refrain lyric over this track.

Rewrite the Hits

Set an original four-line verse/refrain lyric over a track from a hit song.

Write Your Own Song

Create a simple track that has four phrases and one of the chord progressions listed in figure 9.2.

Challenge: A Complete AABA Song

The standard full verse/refrain song has the form of two verse/refrains, then a bridge, then a final verse/refrain. It's often described by letters representing the musical structure: AABA.

Music:	A	A	B	A
Lyric:	Verse 1/ Refrain	Verse 2/Refrain	Bridge	Verse 3/Refrain

To create a complete verse/refrain song, create lyrics to A2, A3, and B—either a moving bridge or a new-key bridge.

SONG 10

Surprising Verse/Refrain ("Those Hands" Version 1)

In these next lessons, you'll learn some of the ways you can create a surprising verse/refrain.

Listen

Hit songs in a surprising verse/refrain form include:

- The Beatles: "And I Love Her," "We Can Work It Out"
- Billy Joel: "Still Rock and Roll to Me,""Just the Way You Are"
- Chuck Berry: "No Particular Place to Go "
- Whitney Houston: "Saving All My Love for You"
- Lionel Richie and Diana Ross: "Endless Love"

- Michael Jackson: "I'll Be There"
- Stevie Wonder: "Living for the City"
- Cream: "Sunshine of Your Love"
- Eric Clapton: "Wonderful Tonight"
- Willie Nelson: "Always on My Mind"
- Paul Simon: "The Sound of Silence"

Lesson 30. Verse/Refrain with Repeated Title

The most common way to create a surprising verse/refrain is to add a phrase to a standard structure, making it five phrases. *Repeat a fourth line title for a fifth phrase.*

Listen

Hit songs in a verse/refrain form with a repeated title include:

- Paul Simon: "Still Crazy After All These Years"
- The Eagles: "After the Thrill Is Gone" (verse 2)
- The Pointer Sisters: "Fire" (last verse)
- Everly Brothers: "All I Have to Do Is Dream"

It looks like this:

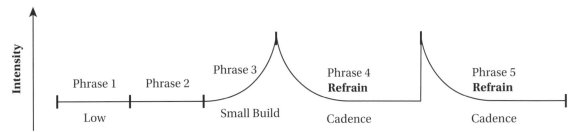

FIG. 10.1. Surprising Verse/Refrain Intensity Flow

Listen to this example, and notice:

- The instrumental hook is up front.

- After the opening repeated progression, the harmony starts a build progression in bar 5.

- The melody also builds in bar 5, using higher notes, shorter phrases, and faster rhymes.

- The melody overlaps with the instrumental hook.

Those Hands
(Version 1)

Jimmy Kachulis

FIG. 10.2. "Those Hands" (Version 1), Full Song Form

Listen again, and notice:

- The first title line is set to a cadence in A minor, suggesting a sadder feeling.

- The *repeated title,* in phrase 5, *is varied musically,* this time set to a full cadence that sounds more emotionally resolved. Varying the repeated title is common in this surprising type of verse/refrain.

WRITING EXERCISES

In each of the following:

- Create a simple four-phrase verse/refrain with the title in the last line, and then repeat it in the fifth phrase.

- When the title repeats, vary it musically.

- Use any type of rhyme scheme.

- Use all the tools you learned to build intensity before the titles and then to emphasize them.

81

Practice

Take the verse/refrain you set over the track in the previous lesson, and repeat the title at the end, or set a new original verse/refrain lyric over this track.

Rewrite the Hits

Set an original verse/refrain lyric over a progression from a hit song.

Write Your Own Song

Set an original verse/refrain lyric over your original chords.

SONG 11

Surprising Verse/Refrain ("Those Hands" Version 2)

This next version of "Those Hands" extends the verse/refrain form.

Lesson 31. Extended Verse/Refrain

The next way to create a surprising verse/refrain is to first create a simple four-line verse and then set the title in the fifth line. But you can use any number of phrases before the title.

Listen

Hit songs in an extended verse/refrain form include:

- Stevie Wonder: "Living for the City"
- Jimi Hendrix Experience: "The Wind Cries Mary"
- Bonnie Raitt: "Nick of Time"
- Rod Stewart: "Forever Young"
- Billy Joel: "It's Still Rock and Roll to Me"
- Whitney Houston: "Saving All My Love for You"
- Sting: "The Russians"
- Bob Dylan: "The Times They Are a-Changin'," "Blowin' in the Wind"
- Kelly Clarkson: "Breakaway"
- Jeff Buckley: "Hallelujah"
- The Rolling Stones: "As Tears Go By"
- Justin Bieber: "Mistletoe"
- Ray Charles: "Hallelujah I Love Her So"
- James Brown: "I Got You (I Feel Good)"
- Elvis Presley: "Can't Help Falling in Love"
- Chuck Berry: "No Particular Place to Go"
- Willie Nelson: "Blue Eyes Cryin' in the Rain"

Listen to this example, and notice:

- The instrumental hook is up front.

- It uses the phrasing (221122) and the rhyme scheme (aabbcc).

- The melody starts building in the second phrase and continues right up until the title.

Those Hands
(Version 2)

Jimmy Kachulis

82

Pop/R&B Ballad

FIG. 11.1. "Those Hands" (Version 2), Full Song Form

Listen again, and notice how it:

- moves to the key of G minor before the title, adding a hint of sadness
- builds intensity in bars 5–6 of the verse, with shorter phrases, faster rhymes, and higher notes, as before
- continues building in bars 7–8 of the verse with even higher notes and a faster bass line
- emphasizes the title with a full cadence to I, and a melodic cadence to Do (B♭)

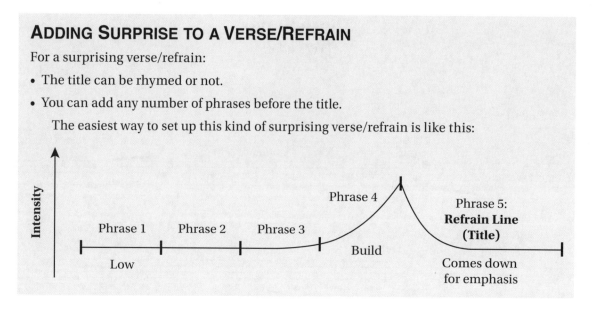

FIG. 11.2. Extended Verse/Refrain Intensity Flow

WRITING EXERCISES

In each of the following, use your tools to build intensity, keep it going until you arrive at the title line, and emphasize the title. Either expand your previous verse/refrain song using these tools or create a new song.

Practice

83

Set an original verse/refrain lyric that has the same phrasing and rhyme scheme as this track.

Rewrite the Hits

Set an original verse/refrain lyric to a track from a hit song.

Write Your Own Song

Set an original lyric to an original progression with an extended verse/refrain form.

Unit IV.

Surprising Forms

What you've learned so far are standard song forms. After you are comfortable creating them, you may feel the need to surprise the audience on a large scale, with a less predictable form. All the surprising forms are based on variations of the forms you learned so far, and they are becoming more and more common.

SONG 12

Combination Form: Verse/Refrain with Chorus ("All I Need Is You")

The verse/refrain with a chorus is a combination form that starts off sounding like an AABA song—that is, a typical verse/refrain. However, after the second verse/refrain (A2), you may decide, for a variety of reasons, to use this surprising form:

- The title needs more emphasis than it gets in the verse/refrain.
- The song might have a bigger audience if you bring in a chorus.

The big differences between this form and a standard AABA song are:

- Instead of a bridge, you create a chorus.
- The song ends with a chorus.

The overall form looks like this:

Music:	A1	A2	Chorus	A3	Chorus
Lyric:	Verse 1/ Refrain	Verse 2/ Refrain	Chorus	Verse 3/ Refrain	Chorus

Listen

Hit songs in this song form include:

- The Beatles: "Let It Be," "All My Loving," "Can't Buy Me Love," "Rain"
- Selena Gomez: "Naturally"
- Willie Nelson: "On the Road Again"
- Justin Bieber: "Mistletoe"
- Jeff Buckley: "Hallelujah"
- Stevie Wonder: "Signed, Sealed, Delivered (I'm Yours)"
- Rod Stewart: "Forever Young"
- Billy Joel: "Only the Good Die Young"
- Percy Sledge: "When a Man Loves a Woman"
- David Guetta: "Without You"
- Kelly Clarkson: "Breakaway"
- Hank Williams: "I Saw the Light"
- Sheryl Crow: "Strong Enough"
- Sting: "Be Still My Beating Heart"
- Bo Diddley, Hank Williams Jr: "You Can't Judge a Book By Looking at the Cover"

You can use any of the verse/refrain and chorus types in this song form.

Lesson 32. Verse/Refrain with a Chorus

You can use any standard or surprising verse/refrain for the verse/refrain with a chorus.

Listen to this example, and notice that this surprising verse/refrain uses:

- a rap verse—another great way to combine rap verse lyrics with a sung chorus

- a surprising phrasing pattern (111122) and rhyme scheme (xaxabb)

- a simple I chord for phrases 1 and 2

84

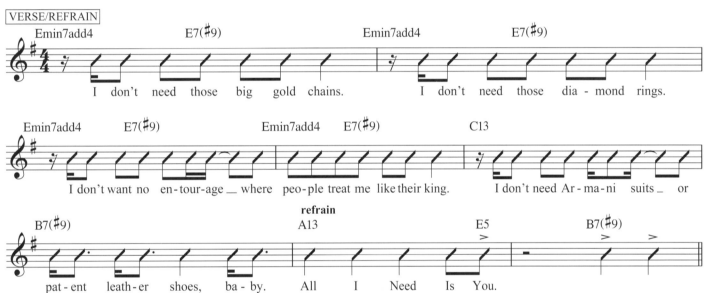

FIG. 12.1. "All I Need Is You" Verse/Refrain

Listen again, and notice how it:

- builds intensity in phrase 3 by moving away from the I chord

- emphasizes the title with longer rhythms, a downbeat ending, and a IV I plagal cadence in a blues key color

- ends on the V chord, to smoothly connect it to the next section

WRITING EXERCISES

As you learned earlier, when using short notes for your verses, prechoruses, and bridges, you can create two versions:

- Version 1: straight rap with standard two pitches, high and low
- Version 2: a melodic, conventional verse, using more pitches

85

Practice

Set an original verse/refrain lyric based on this structure over this track.

Rewrite the Hits

Set an original verse/refrain lyric over a track from a hit song.

Write Your Own Song

Set an original verse/refrain lyric over an original track.

Challenge

A new, contemporary combination form variation is starting to emerge as well. It combines verse/refrain, prechorus, and chorus, and it looks like this:

Verse/Refrain	Prechorus	Chorus

Listen

Hit songs using this new combination include:
- Taylor Swift: "Today Was a Fairytale"
- Adele: "Hello"

Try setting an original lyric and chord progression to a verse/refrain with a prechorus.

Lesson 33. Chorus in Complete Combination Form

You can use any standard or surprising chorus for this form as well. Remember that *the idea here is to make the title more memorable* than it would be in a standard verse/refrain.

Listen to this surprising chorus, and notice how it uses:

- a surprising structure (T–"T")

- two progressions

- tools for emphasis: long notes, rest, long phrases, varied repetition of the title

- a blues melody over Mixolydian chords I and ♭VII

- a pedal part

- a V chord at the end, to build to the last title and connect to the next section

86

FIG. 12.2. "All I Need Is You" Chorus

Now listen to the combination of verse/refrain with a chorus, and notice the sectional contrasts: note lengths, phrase lengths, number of phrases, rhyme scheme, pitches, shapes, and chords, particularly the beginning and ending chords.

All I Need Is You

Jimmy Kachulis

87

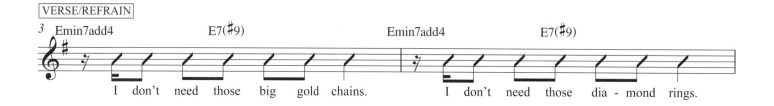

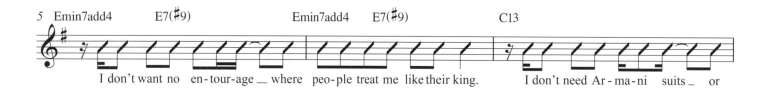

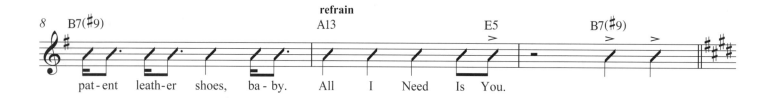

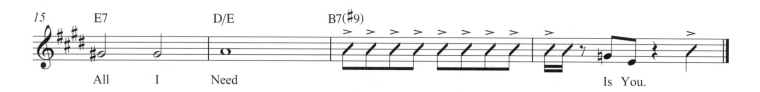

FIG. 12.3. "All I Need Is You" Full Song Form

Listen again, and notice that the simple refrain title at the end of the verse gets even more emphasis when it's used and developed in the following chorus.

WRITING EXERCISES

In each of the following:

- Take any verse/refrain you created in a previous lesson, and create a chorus for it using that title, with or without swing lines.

- Remember, the idea here is to emphasize the title that the audience just heard in the verse/refrain even more.

Practice

88, 89

Set an original chorus lyric over this track. Add this chorus to the verse/refrain created in the previous lesson. You can use the full song form track if you want to create a more complete song.

Rewrite the Hits

Set an original chorus lyric over a progression from a hit song. Add this chorus to the verse/refrain created in the previous lesson.

Write Your Own Song

Set an original chorus lyric over an original progression. Add this chorus to the verse/refrain created in the previous lesson.

CHALLENGE

If you create a standard – – – T chorus that begins away from the I chord, it sounds like a bridge at the beginning and a chorus at the end. Some writers call this a "bridge chorus."

Hit songs with a bridge chorus include:
- Justin Bieber: "U Smile"
- Vince Gill: "Which Bridge to Cross (Which Bridge to Burn)"
- Waylon Jennings: "Between Fathers and Sons"
- Willie Nelson: "On the Road Again"

Try creating a bridge-chorus song based on the verse/refrain form you created for the previous lessons.

Two-Chorus Form ("Celebrity," Version 2, with Two Choruses)

One of the most dramatic song forms of all is a surprising two-chorus form. A second chorus can be added to any simple verse-chorus or verse-prechorus-chorus form. You might decide to use this form when you feel the need for even more emphasis than the song gets with a standard or surprising type.

The two choruses used in this form:

- are different in structure from each other

- can be used separately or together, and in any order

When the two choruses are played back to back, the second chorus can be described in a few ways:

- as a stacked, surprising chorus

- what some refer to as a "post-chorus"

The two chorus song form is also useful for creating different versions of the song for different length mixes, such as a radio friendly mix, the album version, or a club mix.

Lesson 34. Adding a Second Chorus

There are number of ways to create a two-chorus form:

- Listen to a chorus in a verse-chorus song, analyze it, and create a contrasting chorus based on it.

- Create a number of standard and surprising choruses, and sing them in different combinations until you get a combination that feels the most effective.

Listen

Hit songs with two choruses include:

- Kelly Clarkson: "Piece by Piece"

- Katy Perry: "Teenage Dream," "Last Friday Night (T.G.I.F.)"

- John Legend: "All of Me"

- Jess Glynne: "I'll Be There"

- The Beatles: "She Loves You"

Listen to "Celebrity" (version 1), and notice the tools used to contrast and connect the sections in this simple verse-chorus-bridge song.

FIG. 13.1. "Celebrity" (Version 1), Full Song Form

Now listen to this additional, new chorus, and notice how it:

- sounds like a complete chorus in itself (this is crucial)

- uses all the tools you learned to emphasize the title in a dramatic way

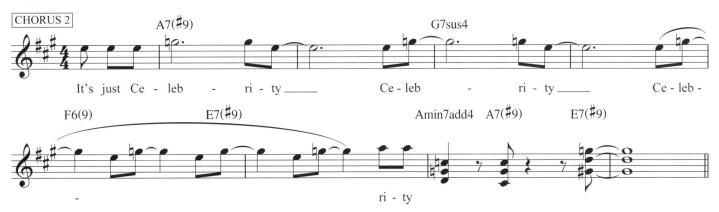

FIG. 13.2. "Celebrity" Second Chorus

There are a number of ways you can set this up. Here are a few hit songs and where the second chorus is located.

1. The Beatles: "She Loves You"

Chorus 1	Verse 1	Chorus 2	Verse 2	Chorus 2	Chorus 1

2. Kelly Clarkson: "Piece by Piece"

Verse 1	Prechorus 1	Chorus 1	
Verse 2	Prechorus 2	Chorus 1	Chorus 2

3. Jess Glynne: "I'll Be There"

Verse 1	Chorus 1	Verse 2	Chorus 1	Chorus 2

4. John Legend: "All of Me" and Katy Perry: "Last Friday Night"

Verse 1	Prechorus 1	Chorus 1	Chorus 2

Listen to the overall flow of this new version of "Celebrity," adding that second chorus, and notice:

- The two choruses are different from each other, melodically and lyrically.

- The two choruses can be heard independently and in any order.

91

Celebrity
(Version 2)

Jimmy Kachulis

Medium Rock/R&B

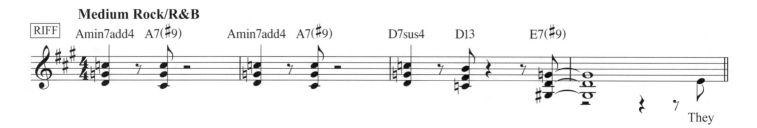

RIFF — Amin7add4 A7(♯9) Amin7add4 A7(♯9) D7sus4 D13 E7(♯9)

They

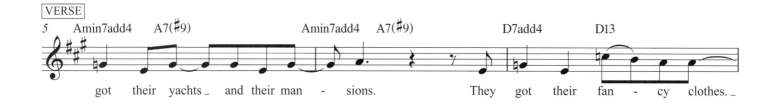

VERSE
5 Amin7add4 A7(♯9) Amin7add4 A7(♯9) D7add4 D13

got their yachts and their man - sions. They got their fan - cy clothes.

8 D7add4 D13 Amin7add4 A7(♯9) Amin7add4 A7(♯9)

They got their stor - ies 'bout their re - hab and how

11 F13 E7(♯9)

ev - 'ry - bod - y knows and it shows. Ce -

CHORUS 1
14 A7(♯9) G7sus4 E7(♯9)

leb - ri - ty, Ce - leb - ri - ty, It ain't noth-in' new. Ce-

18 A7(♯9) G7sus4 E7(♯9)

leb - ri - ty, Ce - leb - ri - ty, It ain't for me and you.

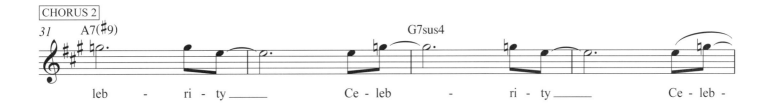

FIG. 13.3. "Celebrity" (Version 2) with Two Choruses, Full Song Form

Verse	Chorus 1	Bridge	Chorus 2

To hear this different effect, compare it with the original version as it was in song 2.

WRITING EXERCISES

In each of the following:

- Keep each chorus short.

- Make each chorus complete in itself.

- Put the song sections together in different ways to see which is the most effective.

92, 93

Practice

Set an original lyric over this track, extending your previous version of your "Song 2" example with a second chorus. You can use the full song form track if you want to create a more complete song.

Rewrite the Hits

Set an original lyric to a hit song with two choruses.

Write Your Own Song

Take a verse-chorus or prechorus song you created previously, and create another chorus that's different than the original one. Try using any of the overall forms described.

APPENDIX A

Key Colors

MAJOR KEY COLORS

Important Chords	Power Progressions	Build Progressions	Full Cadences
I(Maj7), IV(Maj7), V(7)	I IV I IV V I VImin IV V I VImin IImin V I IImin IIImin IV **Bass Line:** 1 7 6 5 4 3 2	V IV V IImin V IImin IIImin IV V	V I IV V I IImin V I VImin V I

I(Maj7)	IImin(7)	IIImin(7)	IV(Maj7)	V(7)	VImin(7)	VII° (min7♭5)
C(Maj7)	Dmin(7)	Emin(7)	F(Maj7)	G(7)	Amin(7)	B° (min7♭5)
D♭(Maj7)	E♭min(7)	Fmin(7)	G♭(Maj7)	A♭(7)	B♭min(7)	C° (min7♭5)
D(Maj7)	Emin(7)	F#min(7)	G(Maj7)	A(7)	Bmin(7)	C#° (min7♭5)
E♭(Maj7)	Fmin(7)	Gmin(7)	A♭(Maj7)	B♭(7)	Cmin(7)	D° (min7♭5)
E(Maj7)	F#min(7)	G#min(7)	A(Maj7)	B(7)	C#min(7)	D#° (min7♭5)
F(Maj7)	Gmin(7)	Amin(7)	B♭(Maj7)	C(7)	Dmin(7)	E° (min7♭5)
G♭(Maj7)	A♭min(7)	B♭min(7)	C♭(Maj7)	D♭(7)	E♭min(7)	F° (min7♭5)
G(Maj7)	Amin(7)	Bmin(7)	C(Maj7)	D(7)	Emin(7)	F#° (min7♭5)
A♭(Maj7)	B♭min(7)	Cmin(7)	D♭(Maj7)	E♭(7)	Fmin(7)	G° (min7♭5)
A(Maj7)	Bmin(7)	D♭min(7)	D(Maj7)	E(7)	F#min(7)	G#° (min7♭5)
B♭(Maj7)	Cmin(7)	Dmin(7)	E♭(Maj7)	F(7)	Gmin(7)	A° (min7♭5)
B(Maj7)	C#min(7)	D#min(7)	E(Maj7)	F#(7)	G#min(7)	A#° (min7♭5)

MINOR KEY COLORS

Important Chords	Power Progressions	Build Progressions	FULL Cadences*
Imin(7), IVmin(7), Vmin(7), ♭VII(7), (V)	Imin IVmin Imin Vmin Imin ♭VII Imin ♭VII ♭VI V Imin ♭VII ♭VI ♭VII	V IImin7♭5 V(7) ♭VI V IVmin V	Vmin Imin ♭VII Imin ♭VI ♭VII Imin V(7) Imin IVmin V(7) Imin ♭VI V(7) Imin

Imin(7)	II° (min7♭5)	♭III(Maj7)	IVmin(7)	Vmin(7)	V(7)*	♭VI(Maj7)	♭VII(7)
Cmin(7)	D° (min7♭5)	E♭(Maj7)	Fmin(7)	Gmin(7)	G(7)	A♭(Maj7)	B♭(7)
C#min(7)	D#° (min7♭5)	E(Maj7)	F#min(7)	G#min(7)	G#(7)	A(Maj7)	B(7)
Dmin(7)	E° (min7♭5)	F(Maj7)	Gmin(7)	Amin(7)	A(7)	B♭(Maj7)	C(7)
E♭min(7)	F° (min7♭5)	G♭(Maj7)	A♭min(7)	B♭min(7)	B♭(7)	C♭(Maj7)	D♭(7)
Emin(7)	F#° (min7♭5)	G(Maj7)	Amin(7)	Bmin(7)	B(7)	C(Maj7)	D(7)
Fmin(7)	G° (min7♭5)	A♭(Maj7)	B♭min(7)	Cmin(7)	C(7)	D♭(Maj7)	E♭(7)
F#min(7)	G#° (min7♭5)	A(Maj7)	Bmin(7)	C#min(7)	C#(7)	D(Maj7)	E(7)
Gmin(7)	A° (min7♭5)	B♭(Maj7)	Cmin(7)	Dmin(7)	D(7)	E♭(Maj7)	F(7)
A♭min(7)	B♭° (min7♭5)	C♭(Maj7)	D♭min(7)	E♭min(7)	E♭(7)	E(Maj7)	G♭(7)
Amin(7)	B° (min7♭5)	C(Maj7)	Dmin(7)	Emin(7)	E(7)	F(Maj7)	G(7)
B♭min(7)	C° (min7♭5)	D♭(Maj7)	E♭min(7)	Fmin(7)	F(7)	G♭(Maj7)	A♭(7)
Bmin(7)	C#° (min7♭5)	D(Maj7)	Emin(7)	F#min(7)	F#(7)	G(Maj7)	A(7)

*V(7) is an optional V chord in any minor key.

MAJOR BLUES KEY COLOR, CHORDS, AND POWER PROGRESSIONS

Note that the *minor* blues key color is primarily used as a melodic tool.

Important Chords	Power Progressions		Build Progressions
I(7,#9), ♭III, IV(7,9), V(7,9,#9), ♭VII	12-Bar Blues: I(7) I(7) I(7) I(7) IV(7) IV(7) I(7) I(7) V(7) IV(7) I(7) I(7)		V(7)

I(7,#9)	♭III*	IV(7,9)	V(7,9,#9)	♭VII
C(7)	E♭	F(7)	G(7)	B♭
C#(7)	E	F#(7)	G#(7)	B
D(7)	F	G(7)	A(7)	C
E♭(7)	G♭	A♭(7)	B♭(7)	C#
E(7)	G	A(7)	B(7)	D
F(7)	A♭	B♭(7)	C(7)	D#
F#(7)	A	B(7)	C#(7)	E
G(7)	B♭	C(7)	D(7)	F
A♭(7)	C♭	D♭(7)	E♭(7)	G♭
A(7)	C	D(7)	E(7)	G
B♭(7)	D♭	E♭(7)	F(7)	A♭
B(7)	D	E(7)	F#(7)	A

*Blue Note

MIXOLYDIAN KEY COLORS

Important Chords	Power Progressions		
I(7,9,13)	I(7,9,13)		
Vmin(7)	I	Vmin	
♭VII(7)	I	♭VII	
	I	♭VII	IV

I(7)	IImin(7)	III°	IV(Maj7)	Vmin(7)	VImin(7)	♭VII(7)
C(7)	Dmin(7)	E°	F(Maj7)	Gmin(7)	Amin(7)	B♭(7)
C#(7)	D#min(7)	F°	F#(Maj7)	G#min(7)	A#min(7)	B(7)
D(7)	Emin(7)	F#°	G(Maj7)	Amin(7)	Bmin(7)	C(7)
E♭(7)	Fmin(7)	G°	A♭(Maj7)	B♭min(7)	Cmin(7)	D♭(7)
E(7)	F#min(7)	G#°	A(Maj7)	Bmin(7)	C#min(7)	D(7)
F(7)	Gmin(7)	A°	B♭(Maj7)	Cmin(7)	Dmin(7)	E♭(7)
F#(7)	G#min(7)	A#°	B(Maj7)	C#min(7)	D#min(7)	E(7)
G(7)	Amin(7)	B°	C(Maj7)	Dmin(7)	Emin(7)	F(7)
A♭(7)	B♭min(7)	C°	D♭(Maj7)	E♭min(7)	Fmin(7)	G♭(7)
A(7)	Bmin(7)	D♭°	D(Maj7)	Emin(7)	F#min(7)	G(7)
B♭(7)	Cmin(7)	D°	E♭(Maj7)	Fmin(7)	Gmin(7)	A♭(7)
B(7)	C#min(7)	D#°	E(Maj7)	F#min(7)	G#min(7)	A(7)

DORIAN KEY COLORS

Important Chords	Power Progressions
Imin(6,7,9), IImin(7), IV or IV(7)	Imin(6,7,9) Imin IImin Imin IV Imin IImin ♭III IImin

Imin(7)	IImin(7)	♭III(Maj7)	IV(7)	Vmin(7)	VI°	♭VII(Maj7)
Cmin(7)	Dmin(7)	E♭(Maj7)	F(7)	Gmin(7)	A°	B♭(Maj7)
C#min(7)	D#min(7)	E(Maj7)	F#(7)	G#min(7)	A#°	B(Maj7)
Dmin(7)	Emin(7)	F(Maj7)	G(7)	Amin(7)	B°	C(Maj7)
E♭min(7)	Fmin(7)	G♭(Maj7)	A♭(7)	B♭min(7)	C°	C#(Maj7)
Emin(7)	F#min(7)	G(Maj7)	A(7)	Bmin(7)	C#°	D(Maj7)
Fmin(7)	Gmin(7)	A♭(Maj7)	B♭(7)	Cmin(7)	D°	D#(Maj7)
F#min(7)	G#min(7)	A(Maj7)	B(7)	C#min(7)	D#°	E(Maj7)
Gmin(7)	Amin(7)	B♭(Maj7)	C(7)	Dmin(7)	E°	F(Maj7)
A♭min(7)	B♭min(7)	C♭(Maj7)	D♭(7)	E♭min(7)	F°	G♭(Maj7)
Amin(7)	Bmin(7)	C(Maj7)	D(7)	Emin(7)	F#°	G(Maj7)
B♭min(7)	Cmin(7)	D♭(Maj7)	E♭(7)	Fmin(7)	G°	A♭(Maj7)
Bmin(7)	C#min(7)	D(Maj7)	E(7)	F#min(7)	G#°	A(Maj7)

Pentatonic/Blues Scales

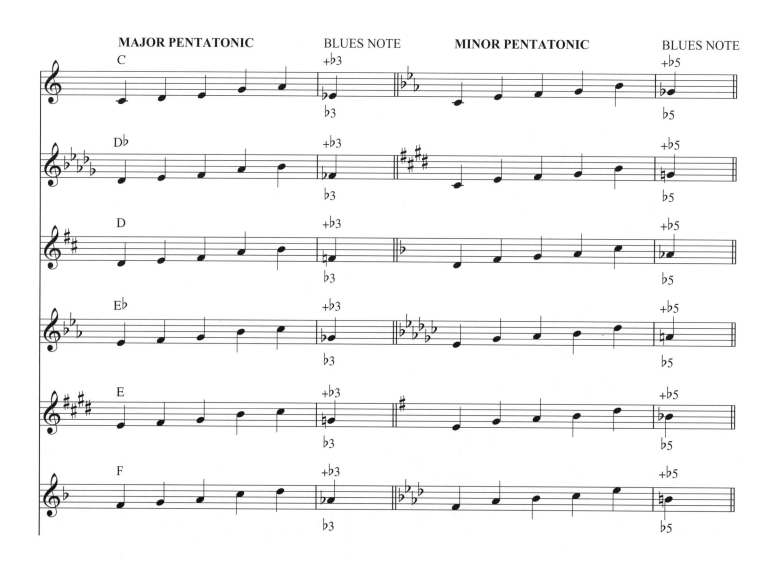

Parallel and Relative Keys

Parallel Keys

C Major	C Minor	C Mixolydian	C Dorian
C#/Db Major	C#/Db Minor	C#/Db Mixolydian	C#/Db Dorian
D Major	D Minor	D Mixolydian	D Dorian
Eb Major	Eb Minor	Eb Mixolydian	Eb Dorian
E Major	E Minor	E Mixolydian	E Dorian
F Major	F Minor	F Mixolydian	F Dorian
F#/Gb Major	F#/Gb Minor	F#/Gb Mixolydian	F#/Gb Dorian
G Major	G Minor	G Mixolydian	G Dorian
Ab Major	Ab Minor	Ab Mixolydian	Ab Dorian
A Major	A Minor	A Mixolydian	A Dorian
Bb Major	Bb Minor	Bb Mixolydian	Bb Dorian
B Major	B Minor	B Mixolydian	B Dorian

Relative Keys

C Major	A Minor	G Mixolydian	D Dorian
Db Major	Bb Minor	Ab Mixolydian	Eb Dorian
D Major	B Minor	A Mixolydian	E Dorian
Eb Major	C Minor	Bb Mixolydian	F Dorian
E Major	C# Minor	B Mixolydian	F# Dorian
F Major	D Minor	C Mixolydian	G Dorian
F#/Gb Major	Eb Minor	C#/Db Mixolydian	Ab Dorian
G Major	E Minor	D Mixolydian	A Dorian
Ab Major	F Minor	Eb Mixolydian	Bb Dorian
A Major	F# Minor	E Mixolydian	B Dorian
Bb Major	G Minor	F Mixolydian	C Dorian
B Major	G# Minor	F# Mixolydian	C# Dorian

ABOUT THE AUTHOR

Jimmy Kachulis is an internationally recognized, award-winning songwriter, composer, author, educator, scholar, and performer. Jimmy's songs have been broadcast internationally on shows and films including *The Sopranos, Touched by an Angel, Jag, All My Children, The Young and the Restless, One Life to Live*, and *The Jamie Foxx Show*. His composition career has run the gamut from concert music blending world music and European forms, to jazz, R&B, and Emmy-award winning TV shows. He has also performed and recorded with legendary R&B, jazz, world music, and early music artists.

Professor Kachulis has created educational material for Berklee College of Music, Berklee Online, and Berklee Press, as well as Tufts University, the Boston Conservatory, and Emerson College. His ethnomusicological research has focused on the music of Africa, India, the Mediterranean, and Southeast Asia.

Songwriters he's trained have written for, among others, Adele, Justin Bieber, Selena Gomez, Alison Krauss, Gwen Stefani, Ryan Adams, *Hamilton*, Trisha Yearwood, Joan Baez, Demi Lovato, Alan Jackson, Taio Cruz, Miranda Lambert, Britney Spears, ZZ Top, Kathy Mattea, Sam Smith, Jimmy Buffet, Imagine Dragons, Faith Hill, Linkin Park, *Dear Evan Hansen*, Emmylou Harris, Gillian Welch, every major publisher and record label, as well as themselves as DIY singer/songwriters.